St. Francis of Assisi

"Poor little rich man"

Allan Procter

Published by

MELROSE BOOKS

An Imprint of Melrose Press Limited
St Thomas Place, Ely
Cambridgeshire
CB7 4GG, UK
www.melrosebooks.com

FIRST EDITION

Copyright © Allan Procter 2006

The Author asserts his moral right to
be identified as the author of this work

Cover designed by Jeremy Kay

ISBN 1 905226 88 8

All rights reserved. No part of this publication may be reproduced,
stored in a retrieval system, or transmitted, in any form or by any means
electronic, mechanical , photocopying, recording or otherwise,
without the prior permission of the publishers.

This book is sold subject to the condition that it shall not,
by way of trade or otherwise, be lent, re-sold, hired out or
otherwise circulated without the publisher's prior consent
in any form of binding or cover other than that in which
it is published and without a similar condition including this
condition being imposed on the subsequent purchaser.

Printed and bound in Great Britain by:
CPI Antony Rowe, Bumpers Farm,
Chippenham, Wiltshire, SN14 6LH, UK

For my Father and Mother, my brothers Bob and
Derek, and for Father Roger
and Carolyn, and my God-children – Aidan,
Charlotte, Emma and Matthew, with love

Statue of St Francis in the Chapel of Caldicott School,
Farnham Royal, Buckinghamshire,
by John Phillips. By kind permission of
the Headmaster Simon Doggart.

Introduction

"Know that God has found no greater sinner than I. He has found no man more vile, none more imperfect. Therefore has He chosen me; so will He show that every good thing comes from Him, the Creator, and not from me, the creature." (St Francis to Brother Masseo)

This is not how we picture Saint Francis in the twenty-first century. He has acquired a veneer of sentimentality, especially because of his love of, and affinity with, animals. He is probably the saint who is loved and respected above all other saints, excepting the Blessed Virgin Mary. We love him today, above all, because he is a man who tried to live like Jesus. In our love of possessions we find it difficult to understand how Francis could have loved "Lady Poverty". Our materialism is the opposite of all that Francis believed. He believed that we could be happier without belongings – all that really mattered to him was God and His great love for His creation. God is love, and with that love comes peace; again and again we hear Francis's constant greeting – "Pax et bonum," peace and goodness. Like all real saints, Francis had a 'bee in his halo'; in his case it was his attitude towards possessions, the importance of "Lady Poverty". The moments in his life when we see him at his most angry are times when he sees his idea of poverty for the Order threatened. There is nothing gentle, meek, and mild about ripping roof tiles off and throwing them at the people down below! Nor in cursing a fellow friar for allowing the Order to own a stone building in Bologna. On both occasions Francis's temper got the better of him, on both occasions he slightly misread the situation, and on both occasions he apologised. We can admire him for that. We admire him, too, because he led by example; anything he asked of his Brothers he was prepared to do; he asked his Brothers to go and preach to the Saracens – to go to almost certain death – and he did the same himself. We learn from him that it is by love, and not by violence, that great things get done in the world in which we live. He is a wonderful and admirable saint because he was the simplest, the most human, and the one who based his life on that of Jesus.

The Beginning

It was the year of our Lord 1182. Pietro Bernardone was glad that he was nearly home. His business trip to France – buying and selling wool and silk cloth – had been very profitable, but he had missed his native Umbria. There the air seemed cleaner and the sunlight brighter, and the stone houses shone a rosy pink, like nowhere else in the world.

Pietro could see his goal, perched halfway up the mountain: his beloved Assisi. Today he was even more impatient than usual to get home because during his months away his wife, Donna Pica, had given birth to a son. The boy had already been baptised in the cathedral of Saint Rufino and had been given the name Giovanni (John). That evening, Donna Pica told her husband that the night that the baby was born she had heard angels singing. Furthermore, when she had taken the boy to be baptised she had been welcomed into the cathedral by an old man with a long white beard who had a serene look on his face. The old man had begged to hold the baby at the font, and after the baptism he signed the sign of the cross on the baby's back. After doing so, he gave the baby back to his mother and then promptly disappeared.

The following months and years were happy ones for the Bernardone family. Giovanni grew up healthy and he developed into a loving, kind and unselfish child. As he learned to talk, his mother, who originally came from Provence, taught him French words and songs. When he chattered to his friends in broken French and sang French songs to them he acquired a nickname – he became known as 'Francesco'– the little Frenchman. This nickname stayed with him for the rest of his life, and eventually he would go down in history as Saint Francis of Assisi.

There was no doubt in the Bernardone household that Francis would follow in his father's footsteps. The boy was not well educated – he learned a little Latin, but could only write with difficulty. (In later life he dictated his letters and signed them with a cross.) Pietro was ambitious for his son and gave him as much money as he wanted. He was well aware that he and his son belonged to the merchant class, but with money Francis was able to associate with the young nobles of the city. He became extravagant and pleasure-seeking, though he never refused to help a beggar. Much to his father's annoyance, Francis often gave away all the money he had on him, and sometimes even gave away some of his own clothes. One story is told of Francis serving a customer in his father's shop when a beggar approached him. Manners meant that Francis had to deal with the customer first, and when he had done so, the beggar had gone away. He left his father's bales of silk and cloth and rushed around the city until he found the man, and gave him money. Then he promised God that never again would he refuse to help a poor man.

A Prisoner

At this time Italy was not united; it was a collection of city-states that were constantly at war with each other. There was a great rivalry between Assisi and the city of Perugia, which was only fifteen miles away. There were many skirmishes between the young men of the two cities. In 1202, the citizens of Assisi were called to fight against their rivals. Francis answered the call, and during the course of the fighting at Ponte San Giovanni he, and several of his companions, were taken prisoner. During the year of their captivity, Francis spent his time keeping up morale and trying to keep his friends unified. In the group was a young man who was very shy and awkward, and who became the butt of many jokes. Francis befriended him, and persuaded the rest of them to accept the young man into their fellowship. When they were released and sent back to Assisi Francis fell gravely ill. The unhealthy prison diet and the lack of exercise contributed to the fever that Francis caught, and he was close to death on more than one occasion. During one bout of fever Francis had a vision of swords, spears, shields, and helmets, all bearing the sign of the cross. He interpreted the meaning of the vision as being that God wanted him to be a Christian knight. Francis recovered, and decided to join the forces of the Pope and fight against the Germans. Pietro gave his son splendid armour and a good war-horse so that he could join the forces of Duke Walter of Brienne. No doubt father and son hoped that Francis would win honour and fame on the battlefield, and that he would be knighted. As he left Assisi Francis boasted, "I shall come back a great prince."

Francis got as far as Spoleto where, it is said, he had another attack of fever. (Some writers suggest that the young nobles in the force decided to put the better-dressed and rather proud Francis "in his place". After his humiliation it is quite possible that he had a feverish night and dreamed about God.) In a vision a voice asked him: "Is it better to follow the master or the servant?" Francis understood that the master was Jesus Christ, and that he was being ordered to return to Assisi, where he would be told what to do. Risking being called a coward, humiliated, and disappointed, Francis returned. He tried to return to his former way of life, but somehow it was not the same. Francis took to walking out of the city to lonely places to think about God and to pray; he also helped more and more beggars, giving away the contents of his purse as well as clothes that he was wearing. His friends accused him of being in love, but Francis began to realise that he had found a bride – not a human bride, but one that he was soon to call "Lady Poverty". "Who is she?" they asked him. "She is someone more beautiful and richer than any one of you can imagine," was Francis's answer.

The Call of God

In the Middle Ages many people were classed as having leprosy. Knowledge of the disease was not as good as now, so many so-called 'lepers' had skin diseases like psoriasis. Any skin disease was feared, so 'lepers' had to keep away from healthy people and live apart. Like everyone around him, Francis feared those who had the disease and kept well away from them. In his will, Francis had written: "When I lived in sin, it was very painful for me to see lepers, but God led me into their midst, and I remained there for a little while. When I left them, that which had seemed to me bitter had become sweet and easy."

One day, Francis met a leper as he rode along the road near the leper hospital of San Salvatore delle Pareti. The man was disfigured in his face and hands. Francis's first reaction was one of horror and disgust, and he pulled his horse away from the man who was begging for alms. Then Francis thought of the way that Jesus had dealt with lepers – with compassion and love – and he felt ashamed. He rode back to the man, gave him all the silver he had, and kissed him on his diseased face and hand. The leper would never have forgotten that act of respect, kindness, and sympathy. Francis then climbed on his horse and rode on. It is said that when he turned to wave goodbye there was no one on the road.

Francis's father was not pleased with his son's behaviour. Francis showed no aspiration to be a knight and he no longer worked in his father's business. The Bishop of Assisi, whom Francis turned to for advice, thought the young man an idle, foolish dreamer. Other people believed that Francis was going mad.

One of the places that Francis used to wander off to, so that he could be alone to think and pray, was a semi-derelict church in a grove of olive trees, on a hillside just outside Assisi. The church was dedicated to Saint Damian and was run by an old priest who was very poor. One day, when Francis was kneeling before the altar in the church, gazing at the Byzantine-style crucifix on the wall behind, he heard a voice that seemed to say: "Go and repair my house, which you see is falling down." Francis saw this religious experience as God calling him, and he took the words literally. The whole Church needed repairing (the gulf was widening between the rich Church and the poor people, and many priests did not act like Jesus and care for the poor, and preach the Gospel to them), but Francis understood that it was the little church of Saint Damian's that he had to repair. Full of joy because he now knew that there was something that God wanted him to do, he rushed to his father's shop. His father was away, but that did not stop Francis from taking some of the bales of cloth and loading them onto a horse. Then he went the ten miles to Folignio and sold the cloth and horse in the market there. After that he trudged the ten miles back, but the old priest at Saint Damian's would not accept the money when he found out where it had come from. He did, however, allow Francis to stay with him, and the young man put the money on a window ledge in the church, hoping that the priest would change his mind.

When Pietro Bernardone returned home he was furious at what Francis had done. Immediately, he went to search for his eldest son. When Francis heard that his father was coming he ran away and hid in a cave, because his father could be a bully at times. After three weeks he decided to face up to his father, so he set out to the shop. By this time his clothes were filthy and torn, his hair was dirty and matted, so as he walked through the city people threw mud and stones at him, calling him "Pazzo" – mad! Pietro was so angry with Francis that he threw him into his cellar. Donna Pica begged for her son's release but Pietro boxed her ears. Eventually, when her husband was away, she helped Francis escape, and he went back to Saint Damian's. A while later Pietro came and asked Francis to leave the district and give up his rights as the eldest son. Francis refused, so his father took the case to the local magistrates and asked them to banish his son. When Francis appeared before them he claimed benefit of clergy – that he was now a servant of the Church so the secular power had no right to try him. Undeterred, Pietro complained to Guido, the Bishop of Assisi, who agreed to hold a public inquiry into the case in his own Great Hall. When he had heard the facts, the Bishop ordered Francis to give back to his father the money that he had got for the cloth and horse. The Bishop reasoned that the money had been stolen, even if it was to be used for a good purpose. If Francis wanted to follow Jesus properly then the first thing to do was to give up worldly possessions. Francis took these words literally; he took off all his clothes and put them in a pile on the floor. Then he said: "Everyone hear and understand; until now I have called Pietro Bernardone my father, but now I will say only, 'Our Father, which art in heaven.'"

Pietro gathered up the clothes and left the hall. By this action Francis showed that he no longer saw rank and wealth as being important; he embraced poverty and trusted that God would provide the basic things he needed to live. The Bishop wrapped his own cloak round Francis and took him into an inner room where he was given a rough coat made of grey homespun cloth which had belonged to the Bishop's gardener. Penniless and homeless, Francis went out into the snow, and as he looked up at the frosty trees he burst into joyous song.

Francis wandered in the countryside, enjoying his freedom and thinking about what he was going to do with his life. Eventually he reached a monastery where he found a job helping the lay brother who acted as cook. For his board and food Francis performed the most menial of tasks: washing pots and pans and helping to prepare and cook the monks' food. He was learning, the hard way, to live a life of poverty and self-denial. A good deal later he left the monastery and went to help lepers, washing them and dressing their sores. Then, after a while, he returned to the old priest at Saint Damian's and declared that he was now ready to rebuild the church.

Thomas of Celano describes Francis for us: "He was of middle height, inclined to shortness; his face was long and prominent, but of cheerful countenance and kindly aspect; his eyes were black, his hair dark, his nose symmetrical, his lips thin and fine, his teeth white and even, his beard black and rather scanty, his hands attenuated with long fingers, and his voice powerful, sweet-toned, clear and sonorous."

The priest welcomed Francis back and shared his home and food with the young man. Francis begged for stones and mortar in the public square in Assisi and then carried what he had been given to Saint Damian's. Francis was not a big, powerful man; on the contrary, he was only just over five feet tall (1.55 metres), and was thin and slight, so he would have found the physical work difficult and extremely tiring. The priest did his best to feed Francis and tried to give him the choice dishes that he knew the young man loved. Francis did not think much about what he was given to eat, but then one day he decided that he had taken too much for granted. Although he was grateful, he decided to beg for his food, too. "I must learn to eat hard fare, as well as do hard work," he said. Many of the people who had known the young Francis called him "mad" and a "fool", but that did not make him change his ways. He was "God's fool", and that was far better than being merely a rich man's son.

After he had finished repairing Saint Damian's, Francis repaired a small chapel dedicated to Saint Peter; then he set to work to repair a third, which was at the foot of the hill on which Assisi is built. This was a small chapel dedicated to Saint Mary of the Portiuncula, or 'little portion' (of land), and belonged to the Benedictine Order. Legend has it that the chapel had originally been built by pilgrims from the Holy Land, to house a relic of the Blessed Virgin Mary. A small portion of forest had been cleared and a few monks had lived there. At the time of Francis there had been no monks there for a very long time and the chapel had fallen into disrepair. The Benedictines had moved to a monastery high up on Mount Subasio. (Later, the little chapel was also known as Sante Maria degli Angeli, or Saint Mary of the Angels. It can be seen, today, inside the great Basilica at Assisi.)

The First Followers

Francis had now run out of churches to repair, so he built himself a small hut next to Saint Mary of the Angels. On Saint Matthias's Day (24 February in Francis's day) a priest from the monastery of Mount Subasio came to celebrate Mass. Francis served at the altar and heard the gospel for the day read from Saint Matthew's Gospel (10 v 7–10):

"Go and preach saying, 'The Kingdom of heaven is at hand!' Heal the sick, raise the dead, cleanse those who suffer from dreaded skin diseases, and cast out demons. You have received freely, so give freely. Do not carry any gold, silver, or brass money in your pockets; do not carry a beggar's bag for the journey or an extra shirt or shoes or a stick. A worker should be worthy of his food."

After the service, in obedience to the Gospel reading, Francis gave away his cloak, took off his shoes, and threw away his staff. Then he took off his leather belt (which probably had a purse hanging on it), and replaced it with a piece of hemp rope. So dressed, he went into the streets of Assisi and began to preach. He was not well educated in scripture, so his sermons were simple and personal, stressing the need for repentance and forgiveness. Some people were impressed by what Francis said, and a small group of followers began to join him.

The first man to join Francis's band was Bernard of Quintavalle, a rich merchant and magistrate. He was middle-aged, and had probably known Francis for a very long time. He invited Francis to stay with him in his house so that he could test if the young man was a genuine follower of Jesus, or just plain mad! During the night Francis used to get up and say his prayers when he thought everyone else was asleep. Bernard used to watch him, and heard Francis repeat again and again, "My God and my all, my God and my all." Bernard had never seen a man so full of praise and thankfulness to God, and it was this that made him decide to follow Francis.

As time went on Francis came to regard Bernard as a dear elder son. He admired Bernard for his great faith and his complete acceptance and love of holy poverty. There is a story that Francis sent Bernard to preach in the university city of Bologna, where the law schools were especially famous. It was a scholarly, cultured, and worldly city that the inexperienced preacher approached with some fear and trepidation. Every day, Bernard went and stood in the marketplace where the children often mocked him because of his shabby and unusual clothes. The young students mocked him, too. Bernard did not retaliate; he just stood still, saying his prayers, bearing witness to his faith. One day he was noticed by one of the university lecturers, Nicholas di Pepoli, who was impressed with Bernard's prayerfulness and his patience with those who mocked and insulted him. He asked him who he was and where he had come from, and Bernard took a piece of paper out of his pocket on which was written the Rule of Francis. Nicholas was amazed by what he read and turned to his friends and said, "I have never heard of so exalted a life as this. The men who live this Rule must be saints. This man is worthy of high honour, because he is a true friend of God." He asked Bernard to stay with him in his own house, and gave him a little house, just outside the city, as a hermitage for the friars to lodge in when they visited Bologna.

Sometime later Bernard turned up unexpectedly at the Portiuncula. He had fled away from the city of learned lawyers. "Send others there, for I cannot stay. I am afraid because the people do me too much honour." In the city where he had been mocked and insulted he was now seen as a saint, and he was afraid that the new respect and love would make him too proud.

Many years later, long after the death of Francis, an old man now, Bernard lay dying. His last words were: "If I could have had a thousand lives, I would have chosen to serve no other master than Christ. Hear my prayer, that you love one another." With a smile on his lips he then died.

The second follower was Peter of Cattaneo, a lay canon of the cathedral and an intelligent and learned lawyer. Whereas Bernard was to give up his possessions, Peter was to give up his ambition of advancement in the Church.

The three men decided that they needed some rules to order their lives, so they made the decision to go to the church of Saint Nicholas in Assisi, hear Mass, and then afterwards they would open the missal on the altar three times to see if God would advise them. After the service they opened the book and Francis read:

"Jesus said to him, 'If you want to be perfect, go and sell all your possessions and give the money to the poor, and you will have treasure in heaven; then come and follow me.'" (Matthew 19 v 21)

When they opened the book the second time Francis read:

"Take nothing with you for the journey: no stick, no beggar's bag, no bread, no money, not even an extra tunic." (Luke 9 v 3)

The third time Francis read:

"Then Jesus said to his disciples, 'If anyone wants to come after me, he must deny himself, take up his cross, and follow me.'" (Matthew 16 v 24)

Overjoyed, Francis said to his two companions, "My brothers, here is our rule for life. Here is the rule for us and for all who wish to join our company. Will you go out and sell all, and we will give the proceeds to the poor?"

Bernard and Peter did not doubt or hesitate; they both went home to put their affairs in order and then followed Francis. Bernard literally gave away all his wealth, in the Piazza San Georgio. It is said that in the crowd that gathered there was a discontented priest named Silvester. He had sold some stones to Francis (for the rebuilding of Saint Damian's) but had not charged the full value of the stones. Now he saw money being given out, so he went up to Francis and complained that he had not been given enough money for his stones. With a great big smile, Francis gave the priest two handfuls of money and asked, "Are you paid enough now, sir priest?"

"I am now paid in full," answered Silvester. In fact he had been paid more than the stones were worth, and after a little thought he realised that he was ashamed of what he had done.

Bernard sold everything that he had and gave all the money away except for a small amount that he used to buy some grey homespun cloth, which was used to clothe Peter and himself. They dressed like Francis, also wearing a hemp cord round their waists. The three of them decided to live in a wattle and daub hut next to a leper hospital. They lived in poverty, and worked in the fields and in the hospital, and sometimes begged for food. Their possessions were few – they had no tables or chairs, and they slept on the ground. Later, the Bishop of Assisi expressed concern at their hard life. Francis's answer was, "If we had any possessions, we would need weapons and laws to defend them. Possessions produce quarrels and lawsuits, and these are the opposite of the love of God and our neighbour. For this reason I and my brothers, who desire only to live in love, are resolved to own no property whatever in this world. We are going to trust completely in God to provide us with a roof at night and food by day."

A little while later, the three men were joined by a fourth, a working man named Egidio. Then came a fifth man, named Giles. Giles was the son of a farmer, and he did not know Francis, though he was a friend of Bernard and Peter. He had been away from Assisi and when he returned he asked where his friends were. "Living down in the valley in a leper hut, with the mad son of Pietro Bernardone," was the contemptuous reply. He was told that they helped the poor and sick, and always seemed happy and cheerful. Giles decided to go and see for himself. He got lost trying to find the hut, which was a mile and a half away from Assisi, so he stopped at a crossroad and prayed for help. Almost at once along came a small young man who was humming to himself. He was dressed in a coarse grey gown. Before he got to Giles he stopped singing and bent down and picked something up. "Little brother," he said, "you should not wander on the path or else you will be crushed by some careless foot." The man was Francis and he had picked up an earthworm, which he then put in a safe place, off the path. Giles asked to join the company and was given permission. "My brother," said Francis, "this is a wonderful thing that has happened to you. You ought to be very proud. If the Emperor had come to Assisi and chosen you out of all its citizens to be his knight and chamberlain, how the others would have envied you! How much more thrilling it is that God has wanted you!"

Giles went with Francis to Assisi to beg for some rough cloth to make him a habit. On the way they met a poor woman begging: "For the love of God, Brother, give me alms," she cried. Francis had vowed that he would never refuse to help someone who asked in the name of God. He had nothing, but he turned to Giles and asked him to give his cloak to the woman. Gladly Giles did so, and we are told that at that moment he felt such joy that he seemed to fly straight to heaven. (Giles became one of the best known and possibly the most holy of Francis's friars. When he was not preaching or helping the poor, he used his farming experience to help with the harvest, or gather olives, or make baskets. Once, in the hot summer, he even carried water and sold it. He was a very practical person who seldom had to beg for his food.)

The next man to join Francis's band was the priest Silvester, who had been profoundly affected by what had happened in the square, when he had asked for more money for the stones that he had supplied to Francis. He was ashamed of his greed, and it had been Francis's smile and laughing, gentle rebuke that had made him decide to join the group.

Francis organised his first mission. He went with Giles,

barefoot and singing lustily, over the mountains, into the Marches of Ancona, and the other three went in the opposite direction. In the village of Poggio Bustone is a white stone in a wall that commemorates Francis's arrival there in 1209; the words written thereon are the first words Francis spoke to the villagers – "Buon giorno, buona gente," which means, 'Good morning, good people.' He was asked to stay with them, which he did for a short time. He climbed the mountain there and lived in a cave near its highest point. It is said that he often meditated there and on one occasion was overcome by a feeling of inadequacy and despair. He dropped to his knees and prayed: "O God, be merciful to me, a sinner. Purify me, purify me, purify me so that I may do Your work. My dearest Lord, I want to love You. My Lord and my God, I give You my heart and my body, and would wish, if I knew how, to do still more for Your love." Then his fear and despair left him and he felt certain that his sins had been forgiven. Later, he returned to Assisi.

Brothers Leo and Rufino

Gradually, other men began to join the little brotherhood. They included four men who supported Francis for the whole of his life. They stayed with him in every sorrow, like, for example, when Francis gave up control of the Order. They were with him on La Verna, they sang to him when he lay dying, and they were loyal to him after his death. The first of these was Brother Leo, who was pure, holy and obedient. Francis called him "Pecorello di Dio" – the Little Lamb of God. Leo wrote down much of what Francis did and became his secretary as well as his chosen confessor and spiritual director. His handwriting was excellent (Francis's was terrible), and later he even made a breviary for Sister Clare.

There are many stories told about Leo. On one occasion Francis was praying and was so lost in prayer that he seemed to be lifted off the ground into the air. Leo went and kissed Francis's feet, and with tears in his eyes said, "My God, have mercy on me, a sinner, and through this holy man let me find grace." When Francis was ill, Leo was one of the friars who nursed him. One night, when Leo was praying by Francis's bed, he had a vision. He saw a broad river that was fast and deep. Several friars, with great burdens on their backs, came down to the river and wanted to get across. There was no ferry or bridge so they waded into the rushing water where, because of their heavy burdens, they all drowned. As Leo stood by the river, deeply saddened by what had happened, another group of friars approached. They had no burdens on their backs, and before Leo could warn them of the danger, they, too, plunged into the water. Without much trouble they got across successfully. The vision faded and Leo woke up by the side of Francis's bed. The next morning he told Francis what he had dreamed and asked what it meant. Francis explained that the raging river was the world and the life we live in it. The friars who drowned were those who were weighed down with earthly cares and possessions. Those who got across the river were glad to be poor and without possessions so that they could follow Christ. They would pass easily from this earthly life to the life eternal.

The second was Brother Rufino, a nobleman who was quiet and shy, and who found meeting other people difficult. When he became a friar, Francis ordered him to go and preach in Assisi. He begged to be let off the task but Francis insisted, saying that if he obeyed then the Holy Spirit would inspire him. Rufino did obey, and he preached well.

Brothers Angelo and Masseo

The third friar was Brother Angelo. Angelo Tancredi was a young, wealthy knight whom Francis met in Rieti. Francis challenged him: "Don't you think that you have worn that sword and belt, and those fine spurs long enough? Change your belt for a rope, your sword for the cross, and your spurs for the dust and stones of the road. We who are soldiers must fight, so come with me and I will make you a knight in the army of Christ."

Some time later, Brother Angelo was put in charge of the hermitage at Monte Casale. It was there that he once made a mistake. In the Rule it is very clearly stated that hospitality is important: "Whosoever comes to the Brothers, friend or enemy, thief or robber, shall be kindly received." One day three robbers came to the hermitage and begged for food. Brother Angelo was not afraid of them, and told them off for their wickedness: "You thieves and cruel murderers! You steal what others have worked for! Would you also insolently take away the alms that have been given to God's servants? Are you not ashamed, you who have respect for neither man nor the God who created you? Go away and do not come here again!"

Francis was staying at the hermitage at the time, but he had been out begging for food when the robbers had come. When he returned with some bread and some wine

Brother Angelo told him what had happened. Expecting praise for his bravery, Angelo was surprised that Francis was not pleased with his behaviour. "Sinners are drawn to God by gentleness rather than reproof. Our master, Christ, says that the people who are well do not need a doctor, the sick do; and many times he ate with sinners. You have broken the rule of charity, Brother Angelo. Therefore, by holy obedience, I order you to take this bread and wine that I have begged, and go and find those robbers, searching over hill and dale. Give them the bread and wine from me and then kneel down before them and confess your fault of cruelty."

Angelo ran off after the robbers and eventually found them. He knelt before them and said, "I confess that I was cruel to refuse you food. Brother Francis sends you this bread and this flask of wine. He begs you to stop doing wicked things, but to repent and fear God."

In amazement, the robbers took the food and began to eat it. The robber leader turned to his companions and said: "This holy friar, because he spoke a few harsh words, which were well deserved, has begged forgiveness and brought us food. We rob our neighbours, we beat and wound travellers, we have even killed people; yet we are not sorry for our sins, nor do we fear God in our hearts. Are not our sins too great for us to have a share in the mercy of God?"

The other robbers felt uncomfortable by what had been said. "What should we do?" one asked. "Let us go to Brother Francis," one of them said. "Perhaps he can give us hope." Angelo and the three robbers returned to the hermitage and the leader spoke to Francis: "Father Francis, we believe that we have been too wicked for God to forgive us, but if you can give us hope we are willing to do what you say and repent of our sins."

Francis replied, "The mercy of God is infinite." Then he spent a long time with them, explaining how Jesus had come into the world to save sinners. The robbers confessed their sins and tried to live honest lives. They became lay brothers and helped the friars, and before they died they all became friars in the Order.

Brother Masseo, the fourth friar, was clever, handsome, amusing, and a good preacher. Perhaps he was just a little too confident and proud, because there is a story of how Francis taught him humility. When the Order was well established Francis used to love to go to the little hermitage of the Carceri, which was about an hour's walk up the mountain from Assisi. He would go there with two or three others to rest and pray quietly. Francis wanted peace and quiet so he told Masseo to act as doorkeeper and cook. Masseo, in other words, was to be the servant of the other friars. Humbly he obeyed, saying, "Father, whatever work you give me, I take it to be wholly the will of God." Francis was pleased and preached a wonderful sermon on humility. After a while, the other Brothers became uncomfortable with the arrangement and asked that the workload should be shared so that Brother Masseo would have time to say his prayers. Wisely, Francis agreed to their request.

Francis loved to tease Masseo. On one occasion, the two Brothers were out on a preaching mission when they came to a crossroad.

"Which way?" asked Masseo.

"The way God wants us to go," answered Francis.

"Which way is that?" was the next question.

"Quite simple," said Francis. "By holy obedience you will spin round and round until I tell you to stop." Francis shut his eyes and at a given moment called on

Masseo to stop. "Which way are you facing?" he asked.

"Towards Siena," was the reply.

"Then it is clearly God's will that we go to Siena," Francis said.

Another story tells us about when Francis and Brother Masseo went out preaching together. One day they had to beg for food so they separated and went down different streets, having agreed to meet later by a stream. When they met up, they laid out what they had been given on a large flat stone. "O, Brother Masseo, we are not worthy of so great a treasure," Francis said, over and over again.

Masseo did not agree. Rather crossly he remarked, "Dearest Father, how can you call this a treasure when there are so many things lacking? We have no tablecloth, no knife, no plates, no bowls, no table, no roof over our heads, and no one to serve us."

Gently Francis answered, "That is why I call it a treasure. We have here no dwelling made by man, but all is prepared for us by God. He has provided us with bread. He has given us this fair stone for a table and this clear stream to satisfy our thirst. So let us pray that He may make us love this treasure of poverty, for He has served us this meal." Then the two Brothers enjoyed their picnic.

When Francis had eleven followers, Guido, the Bishop of Assisi, asked him to go to the Bishop's palace. He explained to Francis that as a layman Francis had no right to preach, so he was technically breaking the laws of the Church. Not for one moment had Francis supposed that copying the way Jesus had lived was illegal in the eyes of the Church. The Bishop suggested that Francis might join the Benedictine Order of monks, but he refused because they owned property. "We are going to trust completely in God to provide us with a roof at night and food by day."

Francis decided to walk to Rome, with his eleven Brothers, and ask for the Pope's blessing on what they were doing. On the walk there it was decided that they would call themselves "Fratres Minores" (the Friars Minor, or the Lesser Brothers). They elected Brother Bernard as their leader after Francis refused, because he was among them "as one who serves".

The Dream of the Pope

In Rome the Pope was Innocent III, probably the most powerful man in the world at that time. He was the son of a high-born Roman lady and a German nobleman, and had become Pope at the age of thirty-seven. Now he was forty-nine. He was everything that Francis was not – highly educated as a lawyer and theologian, aristocratic, powerful, and ambitious. The story goes that he was walking on the terrace of the church of Saint John Lateran when he was approached by a small, ragged, barefoot figure – Francis – the greatest of the great meeting the man who wanted to be the least of the least. The Pope was not pleased to be disturbed by someone he thought was a shepherd or swineherd, or a madman. Peevishly he said, "Go away and roll in the mud with your pigs!"

Francis turned away and went looking for pigs. As luck, or God, would have it, he bumped into the Bishop of Assisi. Guido, who was experienced in the ways of the papal Court, approached a man whom he knew could help Francis – Cardinal John of Saint Paul. The Cardinal talked to Francis and to his companions and suggested that they join an established order of monks like the Benedictines or the Augustinian Canons. Again Francis refused, arguing that they all wished to live as Jesus did, without possessions of any sort. It was agreed that the Cardinal should put the case before a College of

Cardinals – the Curia. "He and his Brothers are simply asking to do what Christ did, and the Apostles after Him, and that is to go about preaching and ministering, while they support themselves with the work of their hands or by the alms of the faithful," he argued. Some Cardinals thought that doing that would be too hard or even impossible. "But these men only want to put into practice the orders that Christ undoubtedly issued to some of His disciples, and if we are saying that they are impossible of fulfilment are we not insulting Him?" the Cardinal retorted. To that there was no answer, so Francis and his companions were called before the Curia to explain in more detail how they wanted to live their lives.

We are told that the Pope had had a dream in which he saw the great church of Saint John Lateran, the mother-church of Rome, falling down, when suddenly a small man, dressed in a hermit's grey robe, rushed forward to prop the building up with his own body. Innocent was troubled by the state of the Church. Perhaps he thought that God was telling him that Francis and his companions had been sent to save the Church of Christ, just as in the dream he had saved the oldest church in the city of Rome. Anyway, the end result was that verbal approval was given, with a promise that if the Brothers were successful then they should return and written authority would be given, too.

"My son," said the Pope, "we have decided to give our approval to your way of life, and our authority to you to preach. Go with the Lord, and as the Lord shall inspire you, preach penitence to all. And if He shall multiply you into a greater fellowship, then you will come to us again, and we will accord you more than this. We shall then commit to you larger powers with more assurance."

St Francis of Assisi

With great joy, Francis and his companions knelt before Pope Innocent and promised him obedience. They had been given a licence to preach penitence, which meant that they were not to touch on questions of dogma. Innocent also ordered that the friars should wear the lesser tonsure, that is to shave the crown of their heads, like a priest or monk, to show that they were under the protection of the Church. "Go out and see what you can do," the Pope said to the leader of the new Order of the Lesser Brothers. It was about this time that Francis was ordained as a deacon – though he never became a priest.

Brothers Guy and Elias

When they returned from Rome the Brothers lived in an "abandoned hovel" and ministered to lepers at a place called Rivo-Torto ('twisted stream'). Other men came to join them. One of these was a young nobleman called Guy of Cortona. When Francis had been preaching in Cortona, Guy had invited him, and the Brothers with him, to stay in his house. When they arrived he had personally washed their feet, and had waited on them at the supper table.

As they left the next day Francis said, "This noble young man who is so thankful to God, so kind and courteous to his neighbours and to the poor, would make a good friar. Courtesy comes from God and is a sister to charity. Gladly would I have this young man in our company."

When Francis returned to Cortona, Guy asked to become a friar and was received into the Order in the church there. He gave away his riches and chose to live in two small caves near Cortona, working and praying with two or three companions.

A second man from Cortona joined the Order – Brother Elias. He was strong, stern, and serious and loved things to be ordered, and he found himself a bit out of place in the carefree company of the other friars. He found it very difficult to embrace a life of poverty and humility, mainly because he had had to work so hard to escape from being poor.

Brothers William and Juniper

Another new recruit was Brother William, who had been a poet and troubadour. In fact, he had been the "King of the Verses" in the Court of the Holy Roman Emperor. He had been visiting a convent where one of his relatives was a sister, and he heard Francis preach. He was so impressed that he left the Court and joined the Order, taking the name Pacifico (The Peaceful).

Brother Juniper was so good that Francis wished that he had "a whole forest of junipers". Sister Clare called him "the plaything of God". Before he became a friar he was a cobbler and he always carried an awl up his sleeve to mend the Brothers' sandals. Juniper was large-hearted and soft-headed! He was absent-minded and eccentric, and got into endless trouble, yet was so humble he never got angry when he was told off. Many stories are told about him. On one occasion he was left in charge of the cooking, with disastrous results! He got it into his head that cooking interrupted prayer time, so it would be a good idea to cook enough to keep the Brothers going for a week or two. He went into Assisi and begged some large pots, some chickens, some vegetables, and some herbs. Then he lit a big fire and cooked everything that he had been given. The chickens still had their feathers, the eggs still had their shells, but they all went into the pots. To Brother Juniper that sort of thing really did not matter. If, when everything was cooked, the Brothers had to pull a feather or two out of the pile on their plates, or deal with egg shells, well that was easy enough. The occasional eggshell would not kill them! When the Brothers returned from their work, they were greatly amused by the sight of Brother Juniper working in the kitchen. The fire was so hot that he had got a wooden board and had tied it on his front to give some protection from the scorching heat. "Brother Juniper is making a wedding feast," they laughed. But their laughter completely died when Juniper served the meal on a huge dish. The food was inedible and had to be thrown away. When they were told that there were several more pans of food in the kitchen they became angry at the huge amount of waste. Brother Juniper realised how foolish he had been and went and hid himself for a day. He was so sorry the Brothers quickly forgave him.

Juniper's simple heart was so full of goodness that he could never refuse to help the needy. When he had nothing to give, he gave away his clothes. Many times he returned with no habit because he had given it to someone who had less to wear than he did. Eventually he was forbidden to give his clothes away. One day he was stopped by a beggar who was almost naked, who asked him for help. "I have nothing but my habit," said Juniper, "and I am not allowed to give it away. But if you take it, I will not stop you!" The beggar did not have to be told a second time, so he stripped Brother Juniper of his habit, and went off. Juniper returned and said, "An honest fellow took it from my back and went off with it."

On another occasion, Brother Juniper was praying in a church in Assisi. The church was well looked after and had many precious things. The sacristan asked Brother

Juniper to look after the church whilst he went off for his lunch. Juniper gladly agreed to do so. A little later a poor woman came in and begged for money for food. The friar had no money; in fact he had nothing of value at all. He looked round the church and noticed a very rich altar frontal that had some small silver bells hanging on it. Forgetting that they were not his to give away, Juniper cut the bells off and told the woman to go and sell them, and buy food for her family. When the sacristan returned he thought that the church had been robbed, but Juniper admitted what he had done. The sacristan was very angry and took the frontal and Brother Juniper to the Father-General of the Order to complain. The Father-General called all the friars together and gave a severe rebuke to Juniper. He spoke so loudly, and for so long, that he practically lost his voice. Juniper accepted that he had been in the wrong. He was determined to do something about the Father-General's hoarseness so he went and begged for some porridge and butter, returned to the Portiuncula, and heated it up. Then, with the hot dish in one hand and a candle in the other he took the porridge to the Father-General. Because it was late the Father-General had to get out of bed, and he was not pleased; he was sleepy and angry at being disturbed, and refused to eat. "In that case it is a pity to waste it," said Juniper, "so do me the favour of holding the candle and I will eat it myself."

The Father-General was so impressed with Juniper's consideration and patience that he was ashamed at his bad temper and said, "If you want to eat it, then we will eat it together." So they ate it all, and Juniper went to bed a happy man.

How the Brothers Lived – The Perfect Friar

Francis was a great judge of character. He knew when to be gentle and when to be harsh. One night, all the friars were woken up by someone shouting, "I am dying!" They all got up and saw a very young friar who was crying. "How are you dying?" they asked him. "I am dying of hunger," was the reply. Francis immediately ordered that any food they had should be put out in front of them all. Then he sat down and began to eat, saying to the frightened young man, "Come and eat with me." Then he beckoned to all the others to sit down and eat as well.

When the food had been eaten Francis preached a short homily: "My dear brothers," he began, "I order each of you to consider his own nature and, if you feel you need more food than some stronger brother, to take it. Beware of too great abstinence, and remember always that our Lord prefers mercy to sacrifice. Besides, we must look after Brother Body, or it will turn melancholy and become a drag on us. After all, if we want it to serve us in work and prayer, we must give it no reasonable cause to murmur. But by all means, if it starts grumbling after receiving a fair ration, let us make the lazy beast feel the spur." Francis called the body "Brother Ass", not in contempt, because he would never have despised an

St Francis of Assisi

ass, but because he liked the image of the body being a good, patient servant, and the soul was the rider.

One morning, Francis got up early because he was worried about one of the oldest Brothers who appeared to be too weak to fast. Waking the Brother, he said, "Come outside with me." He took the old man out into the vineyard and looked for a vine that had excellent grapes. Choosing one, he began to pick bunches of grapes, and then sat down and began to eat them with much enjoyment. Then he ordered the old Brother to sit down with him and help him finish the grapes. (That Brother, to the end of his life, could not tell this story without tears in his eyes.)

To this day, Franciscan friars wear a white cord with three knots in it, to remind them of their three vows of poverty, chastity, and obedience. These three promises were of great importance to Francis, especially "Lady Poverty". At Rivo-Torto there was a young novice who "did hardly pray at all, and worked little, but did eat bravely". Francis judged the man to be too worldly and sent him away. As the Brother was eating a hearty meal, Francis said, "Go your way, Brother Fly, for you eat the labour of your brothers, and are idle in the work of God, like some lazy and barren drone." In other words, he told Brother Fly to buzz off!

There is another story to do with obedience. It is said that two young men came and asked Francis if they could join the Order. Francis was working in the garden and said, "Before I accept you, I want you to do something for me." Stooping down he picked up two cabbage plants and gave one to each of them. Pointing to the freshly dug earth, he said, "I want you to plant a cabbage for me." As the young men stooped to begin their task Francis added, "One more thing; I want you to plant the cabbages upside-down, with the roots up in the air and the leaves in the ground."

One of the men did as Francis asked, but the other questioned Francis's order, saying, "That is the wrong way to plant cabbages! They will never grow like that!"

Francis smiled and said, "I agree with you, but that was not the object of the exercise. The test was one of obedience, and I am sorry to say that you failed." Then he shook hands with the first young man and said, "If you still want to, I welcome you to become a novice in the Order."

"The perfect friar," said Francis, "should have the faith of Brother Bernard and his love of holy poverty, the simplicity and purity of Brother Leo, the courtesy of Brother Angelo, the graciousness and eloquence of Brother Masseo, the patience of Brother Juniper, the charity of Brother Roger. Like Brother Giles his mind should be raised to contemplate God, and like Brother Rufino he should never cease to pray. He should be like Brother John, strong in mind and body to follow Christ, and even as Brother Lucido he should say, 'Our dwelling place is not here but in heaven.'"

The Singing Contest

Francis realised how important it was for the Brothers to retreat from the world to recharge their "spiritual batteries". Peace and quiet, and a time for meditation and prayer, were very important. Life was too hectic at Rivo-Torto, which was a centre for working and preaching friars. "Preaching soils the feet of the soul with dust," he said. With the permission of the Abbot of Subasio, Francis was able to make a hermitage in the foothills of Mount Subasio. It was made in some natural caves which were at the top of a dark gorge, surrounded by a dense wood. He gave it the nickname of "Carceri" which means 'prisons', or cells. Francis often went there and, on one occasion, took part in an endurance contest with a nightingale. Delighted by the bird's song, Francis asked Brother Leo, who was there at the time, to join in the singing. The quiet, shy Leo refused, claiming that he had no great singing voice; so Francis (who loved singing and was quite proud of his voice) went out alone and told the nightingale that he would join in the praises to God, and they would see who could sing the longest. After an hour or two he gave up and declared that the nightingale had easily won the contest.

Francis likened the work at Rivo-Torto and the prayer and meditation at Carceri to the story of Martha and Mary (Luke 10). "Those who wish to live in a hermitage must be three or at most four brothers. And two of them shall be mothers and have the care of the other two. But the mothers shall lead the life of Martha, and the others the life of Mary. The two sons shall each have his own cell where they may pray and sleep. And as soon as the sun has set they shall pray the Compline, and try to maintain silence. And . . . They can go to their mothers, and, if they wish, can beg alms of food from them for the sake of God, like other poor people. And the brothers who are mothers shall guard their sons . . ."

"Brother-Christians"

So Francis and his Brothers settled at Rivo-Torto and helped the lepers who lived nearby. He never called them "lepers"; he called them "our brother-Christians". The first winter was very hard. The small hut really was not big enough for them, and the Brothers often went short of food. Sometimes, one or two of the Brothers would stay outside the hut to give the others more room. When Francis found this out he took some chalk and marked off twelve spaces on the wall. Then he wrote the name of one of the Brothers in each space, so that everyone would know where he was to sleep and say his prayers. They had no chapel so they went to Saint Mary of the Angels, which was not far away. As yet, they had no prayer books, so at prayer time they repeated as many of the prayers and psalms as they could remember.

Now that he had the Pope's permission, Francis was often invited to preach in the cathedral at Assisi. People filled the cathedral to hear him. There was a novelty value at first, but that soon disappeared; his sermons were not learned and full of theology, but appealed to the heart and made people realise that they were sinners and needed to try to do better. Francis and his Brothers were no longer mocked, and people began to respect them.

Evicted by a Donkey

In the following spring, Francis and the Brothers left the hut at Rivo-Torto. Their numbers were growing and the place was not big enough for them all. A local man, who had probably been accustomed to stabling his ass in the hut, resented the presence of the Brothers there. One morning, he drove his ass into the hut whilst the friars were praying silently. "Get in there, long ears," he said, "there's no reason why you should not be comfortable in here, too." To add insult to injury, he had put a piece of grey cloth round the beast and had tied it with a piece of white rope.

Francis was hurt by the man's rudeness, but he did not protest or resist, he merely said, "Come, Brothers, God has called us to preach and to pray, not to keep a hospice for asses! Let us go elsewhere." So they all went, possibly to the Carceri, whilst Francis looked for somewhere else for them to live. He went to Bishop Guido and then to the canons of the cathedral, but neither could help. Then he approached the Abbot of the Benedictine monastery on Mount Subasio. The Abbot suggested that the Brothers use the Portiuncula, with its chapel of Saint Mary and the Angels. They agreed on an annual rent of a basket of fish, and Francis agreed that the little chapel should always be the headquarters of the Order (the caput et mater). The great monastery on Mount Subasio is now a ruin, but every year the friars of the Portiuncula still take a basket of fish to the Benedictine monks in Assisi. Francis's rent is still being paid, as he would wish.

The Brothers built themselves huts, by interweaving branches cut down from the forest, around the chapel. They also planted a hedge, and made a garden, no doubt tended by Giles, who had been a farmer and loved gardening to the end of his long life. Francis asked that a small corner of the garden be kept for flowers, which he loved so much. "Let those who look on them remember the Eternal Sweetness," he said. When a Brother needed to cut wood, Francis insisted that he was not to cut down the whole tree. Some of it had to be left to regrow in the spring. In the winter, Francis insisted that honey and wine be put out in the woods so that the wild bees would not die of want.

The Brothers continued to minister to lepers and to go about preaching. Wherever they went they had to try and find work to do to support themselves. They were never allowed to take money for their work, and they were not allowed to accept more food than they needed. Francis himself worked with his hands. At Greccio they still have the tongs that he used to make wafers for the Mass. He also carved wooden bowls for the friars to use at mealtimes.

Begging was allowed when the friars could not get work. It must have been very hard for those Brothers who had formerly been rich and noble to beg for food. Just as it had been for Francis, it meant a battle with pride. There is a story of a friar who had been into Assisi to beg for food. He came back joyfully, singing loudly, with a large bag of food over his shoulder. Francis ran out and took the heavy sack and kissed the shoulder on which the bag had lain. "Blessed be my Brother who goes readily, seeks alms humbly, and who returns rejoicing," he said.

Often, Francis would suddenly burst out into song, just because he was so happy. He sometimes sang in French, the language of his childhood. Sometimes he would take two sticks, like a jester, and pretend that one stick was a violin and the other a violin bow. Pretending to play the violin, he would sing praises to God. "Let those who belong to the devil hang their heads. We ought to be glad and rejoice in the Lord," he often said.

Sister Clare

Count Favorino Scefi, Lord of Sasso Rosso, was married to the Lady Ortolana, and they had five children: Boso, Penenda, Clare, Agnes, and Beatrice. They had a castle on Subasio and a palazzo in Assisi. As a teenager, Clare (in Italian her name was Chiara, which means 'bright', and later many said that she was like a bright light shining in the dark world) had read *"The Lives of the Saints"* and wanted to become a nun. As a child, she played at rosaries on the floor, using pebbles for beads. We can be sure that there would have been great arguments between Clare and her father, because the Count had already arranged whom his daughter was going to marry. Without doubt, he would have thought that Clare's interest in religion was a passing phase. No doubt, too, that she would have supported Francis in his row with his father. By then Silvester the priest, who was probably related to the Scefis, had joined Francis, as had Rufino, who was almost certainly a cousin, too. Both the Count and his elder son argued against Clare becoming a nun, though it is probable that she would have received quiet support from her mother, and active support from her pious aunt, Bianca Guelfucci. The Count had found a wealthy, noble, young man who was eminently suitable as a husband for Clare, but she had turned him down abruptly, arguing that she had given herself to God and would never marry anyone, ever! The Count swore that she would do as she was told, and the weeping Clare ran to her Aunt Bianca for comfort.

It is certain that the Lady Ortolana, the Lady Bianca, and the young Lady Clare went to the cathedral to hear Francis preach about the joy of giving oneself to God. Francis's words would have reinforced Clare's desire to give herself to God – "His words seemed to her like a flame and his deeds more than human." She persuaded Bianca to take her to see Francis at the Portiuncula. After many meetings, Francis decided that God was calling Clare to be a nun, just as God had called him to be a friar. He promised to accept her into the Order, to "clothe" her in Saint Mary of the Angels, and to place her in a convent until he could sort out how she should live her life. Francis was thrilled at the idea of starting an Order of Sisters. There was, of course, the problem of Count Favorino, and Francis knew that he would remain determined that Clare should marry the young nobleman. "Oh, but she can't do that," said Francis and arranged that Clare should be abducted. On Palm Sunday, 1212, the whole Scefi family went to the cathedral for High Mass. Clare was wearing her best clothes – a scarlet robe, a bejewelled belt, a stiff headdress of white linen, and embroidered shoes. When the time came for the congregation to receive the blessed olive branches, Clare remained in her place, her face buried in her hands, absorbed in prayer. The story goes that Bishop Guido (Francis's confidant, who probably knew what was going to happen) came down from the altar and put an olive branch in Clare's hands.

Late in the evening, Clare escaped from the family house by removing some stones which blocked the back doorway. (This small doorway was probably the one that was used when someone in the family had died; the bricks were removed and the body was taken out to the church and then on to be buried. Clare's old way of life was 'dead', and, just like a dead body, she had left the family home for the last time.) Outside, the Lady Bianca was waiting and the two went in the darkness to the Portiuncula. As they drew near, they saw that Francis had arranged a welcome; all the Brothers came towards them, carrying lighted torches and candles, singing their Palm Sunday praises to God – "Obviaverunt Domino, clamantes et dicentes, Hosanna in excelsis!" Then the friars escorted the ladies into the chapel and during the first Mass of the morning, Francis cut Clare's fine golden hair, robed her in the rough tunic of his Order, and tied a white rope round her waist. Before the altar where Francis had heard the Gospel that decided his life, Clare heard the gospel for Monday in Holy Week, the story of the woman who poured spikenard on Jesus' head as he ate in the house of Simon the leper, in Bethany (Matthew 26). "And Jesus said, 'Let her alone . . . What she has done for me is one of the good works indeed! . . . what she has done will be told also, in remembrance of her.'"

Early in the morning of that Monday in Holy Week, Francis, and some of the Brothers, took Sister Clare to the Benedictine convent of San Paolo, just a short distance from the village of Bastia. It was not long before Count Favorino and most of her family arrived at the nunnery. There was much argument and shouting, but the tearful Clare clung to the altar in the chapel and refused to leave. She vowed that neither threat nor force nor pleading could make her leave the life she had chosen. Her family left and a short while later Francis took her to another convent, St Angelo in Panso. Just over two weeks later, Clare's sister, Agnes (aged fourteen), ran away from home to join her big sister. Favorino and his men (though some writers say the group was led by Favorino's brother, Monaldo) turned up at the nunnery and dragged Agnes out by her hair, beating and kicking her in the process. The story says that Clare prayed and Agnes became too heavy for the men to drag along. Perhaps she had put up such resistance that the chivalrous men just would not fight her anymore; perhaps she had collapsed and they thought that she was dead – we do not know. Agnes crawled back to the convent and was given first aid by the nuns.

It was not long before other women, including Aunt Bianca, came to join the Order called 'The Poor Ladies of Assisi'. (Later, they were to be known as 'The Clarisses' or 'Poor Clares'.) Francis realised that he had to find a home for these ladies who wanted to follow the Rule of his Order. He went to the Abbot of Mount Subasio, who came to the rescue again. He gave Francis the priest's house and chapel of Saint Damian. The Brothers enlarged the house, but the furnishings were of the simplest and barest sort. Clare made herself a small garden, just a narrow space on a terrace walled on three sides, where she grew lilies (the symbol of purity), violets (the symbol of humility), and roses (the symbol of love). The Order was enclosed and the nuns spent their time in prayer, or serving the poor who came to their gates. They also ran a hospital for the sick, and a convalescent home, as well as weaving flax to make fine linen which they embroidered for church use. They wove cloth for the Brothers' habits and in exchange the Brothers supplied the nuns with food (it was considered unseemly and dangerous for women to beg).

After Count Favorino died, the Lady Ortolana and her youngest daughter Beatrice joined the Order, which grew nearly as fast as the Friars Minor. As Abbess, Clare was given a Book of Services copied out by Brother Leo, otherwise she possessed nothing but the clothes she wore. One Pope offered to release her from strict poverty but her reply was, "My Lord, absolve me from my sins, but not from following Christ." The same Pope forbade the Brothers to minister to the nuns, except to take them alms. Clare refused to eat until the order was annulled. Once Clare had been ordered to take her Order under the umbrella of the Benedictines; she refused point blank because she had promised obedience to Francis. She styled herself: "Clare, the unworthy handmaiden of Christ, and a little plant of poverty in the garden of our blessed Father Francis." She gave Popes no peace until they granted her what she called "the privilege of most high poverty". Twenty-seven years after the death of Francis, when Clare lay dying, ministered to by Brothers Leo, Angelo and Juniper, she received a papal bull which read: "The sisters shall own neither house, nor convent, nor anything, but as strangers and pilgrims shall wander through the world, serving the Lord in poverty and humility." Just a few hours after receiving this permission to be a true follower of Francis, she died. Pope Alexander IV made her a saint just two years later, in 1255. Six hundred years after her death her coffin was opened, and the wild flowers which her Sisters had placed in there still gave out a fragrant scent.

Francis turned to Clare when he needed help or advice, and she nursed him when he was dying. There is no doubt that they loved each other deeply in that they were spiritual partners as well as Brother and Sister in the same Order.

Francis and the Animals

On one occasion, Francis went on a preaching tour around the area of Lake Trasimene. It was the period of Lent, when Christians remember the forty days that Jesus spent in the wilderness. Francis decided that he would spend forty days alone on a little wooded island in the lake called Isola Maggiore. The legend says that he took two loaves of bread with him, and at the end of Lent there was still a loaf and a half left. The Gospels say that when Jesus was in the wilderness angels came and ministered to him, but for Francis it was a rabbit that was his companion and comforter. There are many stories that show his affinity with, and love of, animals, which he called his "brothers and sisters". It has already been mentioned, for example, that he picked a worm up off the path to avoid its being trodden on. At the Portiuncula, a lamb used to follow him like a dog and even sometimes followed him into chapel. He befriended a cicada (an insect like a grasshopper), which lived in a fig tree near his cell, and it often came and sat on his hand. Later in his life, when he was at La Verna, he was watched over by a falcon. At Siena, during his last illness, he was given a pheasant that followed him everywhere. Once, at Greccio, a Brother brought him a leveret – a young hare – that had been caught in a snare. The leveret ran straight to Francis and he took it on his lap and stroked it to calm it down. Several times he put it on the ground for it to run away, but it would not leave. In the end the Brother had to take it out into the woods and release it.

On one occasion, Francis stopped a boy who was taking some wild turtledoves to the market to sell them. "Give them to me," he said. "Do not let birds as humble and gentle as these fall into the hands of cruel men who would kill them. Are not faithful souls in the Bible compared to doves?" The boy gave him the birds and they did not fly away. "O my little sisters," he said to them, "why did you let yourselves be caught? Now I will make nests for you so that you can be fruitful and multiply as your Creator ordered you." He made nests for them close to where the friars lived, and the doves laid their eggs and raised their young there. The birds were tame, and friendly with all the Brothers. Larks were his favourite birds because he loved their singing, and their very plain plumage reminded him of the habits of his Orders: "Sister Lark is a humble bird because she goes willingly to the ground to find her food; and flying, she praises God very sweetly like a good Religious," he said. He wanted to petition the Emperor to make a law that nobody should kill or catch his sisters, the larks. He also wanted a law that would make all lords of castles and mayors of towns feed the birds on Christmas Day, so that they would not be hungry on such a holy day.

It was at Alviano that Francis began to preach to a large number of villagers when the twittering of many house martins and swallows disturbed him. The birds were building their nests under the eaves of the houses and making such a noise that Francis could not be heard. "My sisters, the swallows," he said, "It is now time for me to speak, because you have been saying enough all this time. Listen to the Word of God, and be silent until I have finished." To the astonishment of the crowd the birds obeyed, and Francis talked to the people with great joy and conviction.

On one occasion, when Francis was out preaching with Brother Masseo and Brother James, they came across a large flock of birds in some trees, near the village of Bevagna. "Wait for me here," said Francis, "whilst I go and preach to my little sisters, the birds." He got so close to them that his habit brushed against the birds that were pecking on the ground. Francis greeted the birds, "Il Signore vi dia pace," ('The Lord give you peace'). Then he began to preach and all the birds in the trees flew down and listened to what he had to say. "My little sisters, the birds," he said, "You should give great praise to God, your Creator, who has clothed you with feathers and has given you wings to fly. He has given you the freedom to go everywhere and has given you the pure air to live in. You do not sow or reap, but God feeds you and gives you the rivers and fountains to drink from. He has given you the mountains and valleys for your refuge, and the tall trees where you may build your nests; and although you cannot sew nor spin, God clothes you and your children. Surely your Creator loves you very much because He has been so kind to you. Beware then, my little sisters, of the sin of ingratitude, and always make the effort to praise and thank God." The birds bowed their heads as if they were showing their respect and agreement for what had been said. Then Francis blessed them with the sign of the cross and gave them permission to go. The flock soared up into the air and burst into song, filling the sky with their praises, just as Francis had taught them.

The Wolf of Gubbio

Not far from Assisi is the small town of Gubbio. Francis went there with some of his Brothers to preach to the people. It was towards the end of his life, because he did not walk, but rode on a donkey and had a rough piece of sacking thrown over his shoulders. His health had begun to fail and he no longer had the strength to climb the steep mountain tracks. The friars passed some people working in the fields who warned them not to go on because there were wolves about that would attack and kill the donkey, and perhaps even kill the Brothers, too. "I have not harmed my brother, the wolf, that he should want to eat me and Brother Donkey," said Francis. "We will go on. Goodbye, my sons, and fear God." The Brothers arrived safely at Gubbio, where they found that the townsfolk were terror-stricken. One particularly huge and fierce wolf had taken to killing and eating animals, and had even come into the town and killed a defenceless child. Francis immediately decided that he would go and find the wolf and stop it killing people and animals. Everyone, the friars as well, tried to stop him, but he ignored what they were saying, because he believed that the wolf would not hurt him. The wolf's lair was not far from the town, and as Francis approached it alone the wolf ran out to attack him. When the wolf got near to him, Francis made the sign of the cross in the air and said, "Come to me, Brother Wolf. I order you, in the name of Christ, not to hurt me or any other man." Immediately, the wolf stopped baring his teeth and came and lay down at Francis's feet. "Brother Wolf," said Francis, "you have done a lot of harm around here. You have destroyed many of God's creatures without His permission, not only beasts of the field, but man made in the image of God. This means that you deserve to be killed as a thief and murderer. All the folk cry out against you, and the people of this town are your enemies. But I believe that you did this because you were starving, so I would like to make peace between you and the people of Gubbio. If you promise to harm them no more then they will forgive you and will not try to kill you. Do you so promise?" As an answer the wolf bowed his head and put his huge paw into Francis's hand as a sign that he promised. "Brother Wolf, since you have agreed to all of this, I promise that the townsfolk will feed you for the rest of your life. In the name of Christ, Brother Wolf, come back into the town with me and confirm this peace." Francis returned to the town and the wolf trotted along behind him. In the marketplace, he explained the agreement and the people promised that they would feed the wolf. It is said that the wolf lived for two more years and that during that time he wandered from house to house and was fed by townsfolk. When he died of old age he was given an honourable burial. (This story comes from a collection of stories about Francis, some true and some partly true. The collection is called the *Fioretti* or 'Little Flowers of Saint Francis'. Some people believe that Brother Wolf was not a wolf at all, but was a robber whom Francis converted.) This may be the truth, but we cannot be sure. What is certain is that the area around Gubbio did have a problem with wolves at that time, and when workmen dug up the place where Brother Wolf was supposed to be buried they did find a wolf's skull. The tiny church of Saint Francis of Peace marks the cave where the wolf is supposed to have lived after he had been tamed by Francis, and outside the town is the church of Saint Vittorino, which marks the place where Francis and the wolf met for the first time. Perhaps the story is more than a myth.

After his Lenten period on Isola Maggiore, Francis began another preaching tour, this time climbing the mountains to the ancient walled town of Cortona. It was here that Guy sold all that he had, gave the money to the poor, and joined the Order. He chose to live in some caves outside the city for most of the rest of his life, became a priest, and lived a life of contemplation, poverty and selflessness. It was from Cortona, too, that Brother Elias came, and he will be mentioned later on.

The Gift of La Verna

In July 1212, the Christians won a great victory over the Moors at Las Navas in Spain. Francis must have been pleased at the victory but the pleasure would have been tempered with pity for the fallen foe. Francis wanted to win not by force of arms but by the power of love. He realised that violence and punishment never truly win, but that forgiveness and love were the only way to succeed in the long run. He made up his mind to go on a crusade with some of his Brothers, and that the weapons they would use against the leaders of the infidels would be faith, love, gentle persuasion, and patience. If he got martyred then that would not matter – it would be the beginning of a plan, which would eventually work. He set sail for Syria and got shipwrecked on the coast of Slavonia. For several weeks bad storms prevented Francis and the Brothers from going anywhere, but eventually they managed to stow away on a boat returning to Italy. Francis took this experience to mean that God wanted him to carry on working in Italy.

So, in the spring of 1213, Francis began to preach in the hills around Ancona. He climbed up to the castle of Montefeltro where the Lord was holding a festival and tournament to celebrate the knighting of one of his family. Francis was recognised and was asked to preach, and he chose for his text some words from a troubadour's song:

"So great the good that I foresee, that every pain is joy to me." Then he went on to tell the rich, proud people there why he had chosen to give up wealth and follow a life of noble poverty. After the talk, the Duke Orlando dei Cattani, Lord of Chiusi, asked Francis for a private meeting. "Certainly," said Francis, "but first do all your hospitable host expects of you. When the festival is over, we will talk together as long as you like."

After the jousting and feasting the two men met, and the Duke was so impressed by what Francis said that he wanted to help the Order in some way. Then he made this offer: "I own a mountain just above my castle of Chiusi. It is a really wonderful place; its peak dominates all the country for miles around, and the curious thing is that while the peak is covered to its very point with pines and beeches, its sides are split into clefts and chasms. We believe that the earthquake that marked the death of our Lord on the cross split the mountain like that. It seems to me that it would be the perfect place for you and your Brothers when you are in need of solitude, and I want to give it to you. It is called Alvernia." (Alvernia was the old name for La Verna.)

Francis thanked the young Lord for his offer, but, not knowing whether to accept or not, delayed an immediate decision by saying that he would send some friars to look at Alvernia. Francis began to wonder if this was a sign from God; the shipwreck and the offer of La Verna together might mean that God wanted him to give up preaching and instead live a life of solitude. There followed a period of indecision and he returned to the Portiuncula, where he hoped that Jesus would speak to him again. No answer came. Francis became more tired and more discouraged. Eventually he decided to send Brother Masseo to Clare to ask her to pray to God for a solution, after which he was to go to the Carceri and find Silvester and ask him to do the same thing. Francis was very nervous all the time that Masseo was away. When he returned, Francis gestured to him to say nothing. He washed Masseo's feet, as one might do for an honoured guest, and he prepared him a meal and served it with his own hands. Afterwards, he asked Masseo to walk with him in the woods, and when they were away from everyone Francis knelt down and asked, "What does my Lord Jesus Christ tell me to do?" Masseo answered that both Clare and Silvester had given the same answer – that he must go out and preach: "for he was sent into the world for the salvation of souls."

Francis got up straight away and said, "Then let us go forth in the name of God."

The Third Order

Taking Brother Masseo and Brother Angelo with him, Francis did as he had been commanded and went out to preach. With the great weight off his mind, he was happy and confident and his preaching was inspired. In a field outside Cannara, he talked to a large crowd, and everyone there wanted to follow his way of life. Francis immediately realised that it would be impractical to empty a whole village, leaving the crops to rot in the fields and the buildings to fall into decay, so, in a moment of inspiration, he decided to create a Third Order (Tertiaries). These people would stay in the world but not be of it; they would keep enough money to live simply but would give any extra to the poor. They would find time for prayer and would help the sick and the poor. They would refuse to carry weapons or fight against fellow Christians; they would refuse to swear any oaths not approved by the Pope. Many ordinary people joined this Order, as did many that were important or famous. Later, Tertiaries included the Lady Giacoma di Settesoli, a noblewoman of Rome, Orlando, Lord of Chiusi, and Giovanni da Vellita, Lord of Greccio, all people who play important parts in the later life of Francis. After them came: Louis IX, King of France and Saint; John, King of Jerusalem; Agnes, daughter of the King of Bohemia; Elizabeth, daughter of the King of Hungary; Queen

Elizabeth of Portugal; Roger Bacon, philosopher and scholar; the poet Dante; and the explorer Christopher Columbus, to name just a few.

The Brothers left Cannara and walked towards Bevagna. They were near the end of their journey when Francis left his companions and preached to the birds.

The Spread of the Order – Cardinal Ugolino

The annual meeting of most of the friars took place at the Portiuncula at Whitsuntide. It is said that at one of the chapter meetings, Francis was visited by the founder of the Order of Friars Preachers (or Black Friars), Father Dominic Guzman. The Dominican friars were also called "the Lord's watchdogs" – a pun on Dominicans – 'Domini Canes'. The two men got on well together and each respected the other. A story says that they met again in Rome where Dominic asked if Francis would give him the rope he wore around his waist. He said that he wanted to wear it to remind him of the holiest man he had ever met. At first, the humble Francis was reluctant to agree to the request; he did not want so much reverence paid to himself. Eventually, as an act of charity, Francis handed over the rope, which Dominic reverently tied round his own waist. They shook hands lovingly and then went their separate ways.

In 1217, the Chapter organised missions to go all over Italy, and other missions to go to Germany, France, Spain, and Hungary. The Brothers appointed to be in charge of an area were called Provincial Ministers, and Francis told them: "You are to be minister-servants, not masters. Guardians (custodes), and not sergeants. You must tend the brethren as a shepherd tends his sheep.

Let all the minister-servants remember what the Lord says: 'I came not to be ministered to, but to minister.' Let them remember that to them is committed the care of the souls of the brethren, and if any soul is lost through the minister's harshness or bad example, that minister will have to render an account before Our Lord."

Brother Bernard led the mission to Spain. Francis decided that he himself had to go on a mission, too. If his Brothers had to endure great hardship, and perhaps even die, then it was right that he should suffer the same and take the same risks. Francis asked his Brothers to pray for guidance as to where he should go, but when they returned some time later he told them that he had decided to go to France. The argument he used was that the French had a great respect and reverence for the Blessed Sacrament so he felt that he had to go to Provence. Perhaps Provence was a place that he had dreamed of visiting ever since he had heard about it on his mother's knee; after all, it was the area where she had been born and brought up. Francis chose Brother Pacifico to go with him, and they walked north and came to Florence. It was there that Francis met Ugolino, Cardinal Bishop of Ostia.

Ugolino was seventy years old when he met Francis. He was everything that Francis was not. He was tall and handsome, an aristocrat, and a nephew of Pope Innocent III. Furthermore, he was a scholar, a great organiser, and totally practical and organised. He was a force to be reckoned with, and expected those who met him to be respectful and obedient. Ugolino decided to organise the Brothers Minor because Cardinal John of Saint Paul had died and the Order needed a Cardinal Protector. He was ambitious for the Order and wanted to use it as a spiritual force in the world, and one way he could do that was to promote Brothers to high positions in the Church. He summoned Francis to a meeting, and after a long discussion Francis came out grateful for the Cardinal's support and goodwill. Ugolino also persuaded him against going to France, arguing gently that Francis was needed in Italy, and also, a visit to France was just a little self-indulgent.

All the missions to the various countries failed except the one led by Brother Bernard to Spain. The main problem was one of communication – the Brothers did not know the languages and dialects of the areas they went to. This led to many misunderstandings and in Germany, France, Portugal, and Hungary the Brothers were mocked, badly treated, and sometimes beaten up. Their ragged appearance sometimes made people believe that they were rogues and vagabonds, and at other times they were taken to be Albigensian heretics. On their return, some of the disillusioned Brothers blamed Francis for their failure, arguing that he had set them on an impossible task. There began a period of strife and argument within the Order. Some of the provincial ministers wanted to discipline and punish the Brothers in their charge because they found that, unlike Francis, they could not rule by force of personality alone. Some of the Brothers wanted more security – they wanted to own property in common and to live more like monks, in a monastery, with a more regulated routine. Others wanted to study and learn more – to follow the example of the educated Dominicans. That would need books and libraries, which the Order did not have. All these malcontents turned to Cardinal Ugolino and asked him to persuade Francis to relax his rule so that changes could be made.

Perfect Joy

Francis realised that his Order had grown so large that many of the Brothers did not understand what he was trying to do and how he was trying to do it. Many of the Brothers did not know Francis personally. He knew that his way of doing things was the right way, but he began to lose confidence in himself as a leader. He became more and more depressed. After one particular depressing meeting with the Cardinal in Perugia, Francis was walking back to Assisi accompanied by Brother Leo. He spent a long time thinking about the things that were going wrong, and about the things that made him happy and sad. As they climbed the hill to the town of Collestrada, the two were caught in a blizzard.

Brother Leo was walking in front, his cowl pulled tightly round his lowered head, when Francis shouted out to him, "O Brother Leo, though the Friars Minor give a great example of holiness in every land, perfect joy is not to be found in this. Note this well and write it down." Walking on, Francis called out a second time, "Even though the Friars Minor give sight to the blind, and heal the paralysed, and give hearing to the deaf and speech to the dumb; even though they cast out demons and raise the dead to life, write that perfect joy is not to be found there." Puzzled, Brother Leo said nothing, and they walked on. Then Francis spoke again: "O Brother

Leo, though the Friars Minor should know all languages and all sciences and all scriptures; though they could prophesy and predict the future and know the secrets of consciences and souls; write that perfect joy is not found there." They walked on and Francis said, "Brother Leo, Little Lamb of God, even if the Friars Minor spoke with the tongues of angels, and knew the movements of all the stars, and understood the ways of birds, animals, and fish, write that even this is not perfect joy." Again there was silence for a while, and then Francis said, "O Brother Leo, though the Friars Minor could preach so well that they should convert every unbeliever to Christ, write that perfect joy is not to be found there."

On the two men went, and then Leo, mystified and wondering asked, "Father, I beg you, for God's sake, tell me where is perfect joy to be found?"

Then Francis answered, "Soon we will come to Saint Mary of the Angels. We are wet through with the rain, we are freezing with the cold, muddy, and dying of hunger. Suppose that when we knock on the door, Brother Doorkeeper comes in a rage and asks angrily, 'Who are you?' and we reply, 'We are two of your friars.' Suppose then he says, 'You are lying! You are two rogues who travel around stealing from the poor. Clear off!' He does not let us in, and leaves us outside hungry and cold in the snow and rain. Suppose we knock again and the Doorkeeper comes out and beats us with a big stick. If we endure such treatment without complaining or moaning, if we suffer patiently, with love and gladness, thinking of the suffering of the Blessed Christ, then write, Brother Leo, that that is perfect joy. For the greatest gift that Christ gives is the overcoming of self."

Friction in the Order

Francis felt very strongly that at the heart of his Order was the pursuit of poverty – "Lady Poverty" – that owning things led to selfishness, materialism, and quarrels. He wanted to convert the world by example, showing how Jesus had lived, rather than just preaching. Just as Jesus had not controlled his disciples by punishing them, he did not want punishment in his Order. He did not encourage book learning because he believed that that sort of learning was not wisdom, neither was it knowledge, because facts had to be experienced to be known. He sincerely believed that: "A man's knowledge is as great as his deeds." Many people pursued knowledge for self-advancement. He accepted learned men into his Order, scholars like Brother Peter Cataneo and Brother Gregory of Naples, and appointed them to high positions in the Order. He respected those who divorced learning from pride, like Bishop Antony of Padua, whom he called "Brother Antony, my bishop". In his will, Francis wrote: "All theologians and those who serve us with God's word, we should honour and revere." He wanted to protect unlearned Brothers from pride, jealousy, and separation, because they had joined the Order to perfect themselves in love, not in learning. People could argue against learned arguments, but there could be no argument against a life of love; in Francis's own words:

"Not by what a Brother Minor argues will the people be won, but by what he is."

Francis explained his attitude towards learning to the Brothers Leo, Rufino and Angelo: "My best beloved, there are many friars who place all their study and care in acquiring knowledge, leaving their holy vocation, and wandering out of the way of humility and prayer. But those whom they think they have converted by their knowledge and their preaching, the Lord has really taught by the lives of holy, poor, humble, and simple friars, though they do not know that they have done it. These are my Knights of the Round Table."

Once, a novice asked Francis if he might own a Psalter. With a smile Francis replied, "And after you have got your Psalter, you will desire a breviary, and you will think yourself a great prelate instead of a Brother Minor, and you will sit on a throne and call to your brother, 'Bring me my breviary!' Brother, I also was tempted to have books, but when I wanted to know the will of God I took up a book in which the Gospel of the Lord was written, and I read, 'To you is given the knowledge of the mysteries of the Kingdom, but to others in parables.' What have I to do with books? O my brethren, all we need do is to pray."

One day, Francis was visited by a learned Dominican, a Doctor of Divinity, who wanted a verse from the prophet Ezekiel explained: "If you speak not to warn the wicked from his wicked ways, his blood I will require at your hands." The Doctor said that he knew some wicked people and thought it about time that they were warned. Francis told him to stop being silly. The Doctor insisted that he had heard many learned people talk about the passage and that it clearly meant that if you did not warn the wicked then all sorts of evils would be visited on you by God. "No," said Francis, "I take the sense to be this. The servant of God should so burn with holiness that he becomes an example to the others. His splendour and the perfume of his name should be enough to warn the wicked of their iniquities." The Doctor went away slowly, muttering something about Francis's theology being "like to the flying eagle" whilst the learned theologian "crawled with his belly on the earth".

Francis's Order had grown so much that Cardinal Ugolino arranged for Francis to preach to the Pope and cardinals, to both impress and gain influence. The Cardinal forced him to prepare a sermon and learn it by heart. Francis had always preached from the heart, without preparation, so this new way of doing things made him nervous and he felt a sham. "Preaching soils the feet of the soul with dust." When the time for the sermon came, both men were very nervous. Thomas of Celano says that the Cardinal was "in an agony of suspense, praying to God with all his might that the simplicity of the blessed man might not be despised". Francis forgot every word of the prepared sermon! Instead he preached from the heart – a stuttering, gesticulating appeal. Some of his distinguished listeners were impressed, others amused, and some were disturbed and disapproving.

The Chapter of the Mats

Francis left Rome and went on a new preaching tour. He returned to Assisi in late May for the Whitsuntide Chapter of 1219 – the Chapter Storearum, or 'Chapter of the Mats'. Five thousand of the Brothers had journeyed from all over Italy, from France and from Spain, to attend the meeting. They camped round the Portiuncula and each group made a sun-shelter that had a roof of woven reeds, on poles. From a distance, it looked like a city of mats. When Francis returned he found that a new stone building had been built next to the Chapel of Saint Mary and the Angels. He was furious – he had always been against friars living in permanent buildings, and he assumed that the Brothers had built it in his absence, without his permission. He lost his temper and, with some of his loyal friars, he climbed onto the roof and began ripping off the tiles and throwing them down. A crowd of friars and townspeople watched in amazement. Some men-at-arms who had been sent to police the people shouted to Francis to stop. They explained to him that the building had been erected by the Commune of Assisi to house all the visiting Brothers. Francis was touched by the goodwill of the Commune, distressed by his own impatience, and relieved that the Brothers had not disobeyed him. He stopped destroying the building, saying, "If you say this house is yours, I will touch it no more."

Just as Francis had made no arrangements for the Brothers' accommodation, he had made no arrangements for feeding them! He trusted that the Lord would provide, and in the shape of the good people of Assisi, Bastia, Cannara, and all the surrounding districts, He did! Donkeys and mules, loaded down with bread, cheese, wine, beans, peas, bowls, jugs, napkins, knives, and much, much more, began to arrive at the Portiuncula. Cardinal Ugolino made his stately way to preside over the meeting and all the Brothers went out in procession, bareheaded and barefoot, to escort him to Saint Mary of the Angels. The Cardinal was so moved by his reception that he dismounted, took off his fine cloak and shoes, and walked in cassock and bare feet behind the Brothers. In Saint Mary's he sang the Whit Sunday Mass, and Francis acted as deacon and preached to the whole Chapter. He preached about the things that were really important to him: of obedience to the Pope, of love for one another, of prayer, patience and purity of life, and most of all, of the importance of holy poverty. At the conference afterwards, Francis asked for volunteers to go and preach to the Saracens – a mission that would almost certainly end in martyrdom. Large numbers of the Brothers offered to go and Francis said to them: "Dearest sons, so that you can better fulfil God's will, see that there is peace and unity among you, and invincible charity; be patient in tribulation, be humble in success. Copy Christ in poverty, for He was born poor and lived in poverty and died in poverty. And this I beg of you that you always have the sufferings of our Lord before your eyes, so that you will want to suffer for Him." The Brothers asked for his prayers and his blessing. They fell on their knees and he blessed them: "The blessing of God come upon you as it came upon the Apostles. And fear not, for the Lord is with you and will fight for you."

Not all went smoothly at the Chapter of the Mats. Francis was deeply upset when some of the Brothers went to Cardinal Ugolino and asked him to try and persuade Francis to make their Rule, the way they lived, the same as Saint Benedict or Saint Augustine. When the Cardinal put the request forward, Francis said nothing; he led Ugolino by the hand to the conference and said: "My Brothers, my Brothers, the Lord called me by the way of simplicity. And, therefore, I desire that you speak not to me of Saint Augustine, Saint Benedict or Saint Bernard, nor of any Rule of life except that which was shown to me by the Lord. For me, the only rule is the form of life which God in His mercy has shown to me and bestowed on me. God made known to me that I was to behave with a madness that the world knew nothing of, and that such madness was to be all the learning that we were to have. May God confound your learning and your wisdom. May He send evil spirits to punish you, and you shall return to your own place, whether you will or no, and curses shall be upon you."

Near the end of the Chapter Francis announced that he was going to preach to the Saracens. He announced his intention of going to join the crusading army that was now encamped outside Damietta. As usual, he wanted to lead from the front; he wanted to do what he had asked others to do. This time the Cardinal was unable to stop him.

On Crusade

Towards the end of June, 1219, Francis set sail from Ancona with about a dozen friars. Many Brothers had wanted to go with their leader but there was not enough room on the transport ships for all of them. Francis knew that if he chose who went with him then feelings would be hurt, so he got a small boy to point at twelve of the Brothers and they were the ones who went with him. Peter Cattaneo, Illuminato, Leonard of Assisi, Barbaro, and seven or eight others were chosen. When the ships docked at Saint Jean d'Acre (Acre today), they were met by the Provincial Minister for the Brothers Minor in Syria, Brother Elias Bombarone. (Brother Elias's father had been a mattress-maker and his mother was a woman of Assisi. Elias had been born and brought up in Beviglia, where he carried on the trade of his father. He was intelligent, and learnt enough to act as a schoolmaster to the poorer boys of Assisi. Later, he attended the university in Bologna, where he supported himself by working as a scriptor. After university, he went to Cortona which was where he met Francis, who had just finished his period of solitude on Isola Maggiore. Elias became a friar, and through hard work, efficiency, and ambition, rose into one of the high positions in the Order. Even at that time many saw him as the natural successor of Francis.) The men spent a few days together and then Francis and his friars set sail for Damietta, in the Nile delta. There he preached to the crusaders. Francis was upset by the wickedness of the crusaders; he had expected to find an army of Arthurian knights, but instead, found a rabble of drunkards, lechers, and looters.

On 29 August the Crusaders began a new offensive on Damietta. It failed, and at the end of the day there were between five and six thousand Christians dead. Force had failed, so Francis decided to try love. With Brother Illuminato, he walked through the Crusaders' camp, out into no-man's-land. The Crusaders saw it as suicide – the Sultan had offered to buy Christian heads at one gold coin apiece. Francis gave encouragement to Brother Illuminato by quoting his favourite maxim: "Cast your care upon God, and He will protect you." As they walked on the friars came across two lambs. Francis saw this as a sign from God, and with a beaming smile encouraged his companion by saying: "Put your trust in the Lord, Brother. He is sending us out as sheep into the midst of wolves!" Near the enemy lines they were captured, and although not killed, they were handled roughly. They were tied up and beaten, all the time Francis calling out, "Soldan, Soldan," meaning that he wanted to be taken to the Sultan. Eventually they found themselves in the presence of Malik-al-Kamil, King of Syria and Egypt. The Sultan was impressed by the bravery of the two friars and, through interpreters, he discussed religion with them over several days. On one occasion he tested Francis. He had a carpet with a pattern of crosses placed before his throne. He reasoned that if Francis walked on the crosses he insulted his own religion, if he refused to walk on the carpet then he insulted his host. Francis noticed the carpet, and, with no hesitation at all, walked on it. "You have trodden the sign of your religion underfoot!" the Sultan remarked.

"Sir," said Francis, "there were three crosses on Calvary. One belonged to the Saviour of the world, and the other two to two robbers. Ours is the true cross, so I can only assume that yours . . ."

The Sultan laughed and suggested that Francis should remain permanently at his Court. "This I will gladly do," answered Francis, "if you and your people become Christians." Although the Sultan was impressed with Francis, he would not change his religion, so Francis suggested a test to see which religion was the true one. He suggested ordeal by fire. He wanted a huge fire to be made that he and the priests of Islam would walk through. The true God would protect His own. The Sultan refused; he knew that his priests would not dare to face the fire. As Francis was speaking the Sultan had noticed one of his priests edging away quietly. Francis then offered to walk through the fire alone. If he came through unharmed then the Sultan was to become a Christian; if he was burnt then it was because he (Francis) was a sinner. Again, the Sultan refused, but he was impressed enough to ask Francis to pray for him, that God would show him the truth. He offered Francis many presents, as well as money to spend on churches and on the poor. To his amazement, Francis refused them all. The Sultan gave the two friars a safe conduct back to the Christian lines, as well as written permission to visit all the holy places in Israel. The mission had failed.

Just a while later the Crusaders attacked Damietta again. This time they were successful, and there was much butchery, looting, and rape. Francis left for the Holy Land. He spent a long time visiting the Holy Places, following in the footsteps of Jesus. Then he returned to St Jean d'Acre and once more enjoyed the hospitality of Brother Elias. Brother Peter Cattaneo was there to welcome him, too. Francis was having trouble with his eyes – affected by the bright sun and the dust of the Holy Land.

One day a lay brother, Brother Stephen, arrived to see Francis. The news he brought was bad. He had been sent, secretly, to tell Francis that the Order was badly split, and that those who loved and supported him begged him to return to Italy as soon as possible. The two Vicars-General that Francis had left in charge of the Order, under the influence of Cardinal Ugolino, were changing the Rule. They were going to build large stone convents where the Brothers would live like the Benedictine or Augustinian monks; there was to be a new calendar with regulated fast days; there was to be enforced obedience to the changes with harsh punishments for those who did not obey. In fact, already, some of the friars who had remained loyal to the original Rule of Francis had been expelled from the Order. Ugolino himself had written a new Rule for the Sisters of St Damian's, turning them into what amounted to a strict Benedictine Order. Francis and Brother Peter were sitting down for a meal when Brother Stephen had arrived. He showed them a copy of the new Rule, which Francis read at the table. According to the new Rule it was a day of abstinence from meat.

"What are we going to do?" asked Francis.

"We are going to do what you say," replied Brother Peter, "because you are our authority."

"Then, in accordance with the Holy Gospel, let us eat what has been set before us," said Francis, and he picked up some meat and ate it.

The Curse in Bologna

A few days later, with several of the Brothers, including Elias, Francis sailed to Venice. He was depressed and upset by what had happened in Italy, he was ill, and he was worried about his eyes. From Venice, the friars travelled to Bologna. There Francis learned that the Minister Provincial of Lombardy, Brother Peter Stacia, with the encouragement of Cardinal Ugolino, had collected huge sums of money and had built a splendid convent for the Brothers. It was to be a kind of theological college and legal school attached to the university, and was called 'The House of the Brothers'. It represented everything that Francis had fought against. It was a concrete insult to what he believed in – poverty, humility and simplicity, so he refused to go into it, and lodged with the Dominicans instead. Francis summoned Brother Peter Stacia to him and solemnly called down Heaven's curse upon him, as well as ordering all the Brothers in that house of sin to do heavy penance. All this from a man who passionately believed in forgiveness and mercy! A Dominican friar begged Francis to be more gentle with his children and after an hour he remitted the penance, but commanded the Brothers, in the name of holy obedience, to leave the House. Cardinal Ugolino, who was also in Bologna, had to use all his tact and diplomacy to explain that the Brothers did not own the House, but that he, the

Cardinal, was its registered owner. Francis accepted the excuse and left Bologna, knowing full well that force and retribution was no long-term answer to the problem. He also realised that the Order had moved out of his control; he was wanted as a spiritual figurehead, but it needed a more practical and down-to-earth person to control it. "It is not for me to act the sergeant of the Lord," he remarked. "If I am not able to correct and amend them by preaching and admonition and example, I will not become an executioner, punishing and flogging them like the magistrates of this world."

Resignation

There followed a long period of mental and spiritual disquiet for Francis. He was also having trouble with his eyes. At the Michaelmas Chapter of 1220 he announced his resignation as leader of the Order and his appointment of Brother Peter Cataneo as Vicar General. Francis had had a dream of a little black hen that had had so many chicks she could not keep them all under her wings. A hen with bigger wings was needed! He saw this as a parallel to his predicament. He was the hen, and the chicks were the Brothers in his Order. Sheer numbers meant that he could no longer care for all of them. A bigger, stronger leader was needed. "I am that little hen," he said. "I am small in stature and black in my nature. The Lord, in His mercy, has given me many sons whom I shall not be able to protect in my own strength." Francis told the Brothers at the Chapter, "From now on I am dead to you, but here is Brother Peter Cataneo, whom both you and I will obey." He bowed to Brother Peter and promised him obedience and reverence. As many of the Brothers wept, Francis raised his eyes to heaven and prayed: "Lord, I return to You this family which You have given into my care. Now, as You know, most sweet Jesus, I no longer have the strength or the ability to keep on caring for them. I confide them, therefore, to the Ministers. May they be responsible before You at the Day of Judgement, if any Brother, by their negligence or bad example, or by a too severe discipline, should wander away." He told them that he was going to go away into solitude to see if he could amend the Rule in the interests of peace and harmony, and that he would take Brother Caesar of Speyer, a wise and learned man, to help him.

There followed what Saint John of the Cross called "the dark night of the soul". The Order that Francis had founded, nurtured and loved, was not his anymore, and it began to change in ways he did not approve of. A core of Brothers supported him, including Brother Bernard, Brother Leo, Brother Masseo, Brother Giles, Brother Angelo, and, of course, Sister Clare in Saint Damian's. It was suggested that he split the Order, but he refused. Francis retreated to the lonely little hermitage on Mount Rainerio, above the Rietan Valley. He spent a long time praying in the little chapel there, built with his own hands, and dedicated to Saint Mary Magdalene. He tried to amend his Rule without anger and thoughts of revenge, so that what he wanted would not split the Brotherhood.

Brother Peter Cataneo might have been a bridge between Francis and the new Order, but unfortunately he died soon after being appointed as Vicar General. Brother Elias was appointed in his place. Francis wrote to Brother Elias begging him to treat those Brothers who disagreed with him (Elias) with compassion and love rather than with condemnation and harshness. "To Brother Elias, Minister. The Lord bless you. I speak to you as I am able concerning the condition of your soul. If there are people, whether Brothers or not, who hinder you in loving the Lord God, yet you should count all such trials as favours. And let this be a command to you from the Lord and from me . . . Love those who do such things to you . . . And by this I shall know that you love God and me, His servant and yours . . . Keep this letter by you so that it may be better observed." Elias regarded this advice as impractical, so he ignored it. Like Cardinal Ugolino, Brother Elias believed in order and strict discipline. Although he rejected Francis's emphasis on patience and leniency, he did not lose his love and respect for Francis himself. (In the long months of Francis's last illness, Elias cared for him "in loco matris", like a mother, [Francis's own words]. After Francis had died, Elias built a huge church to house the body, even though Francis had ordered his followers not to build fine churches. The church of San Francesco is a monument to Brother Elias rather than to "Il Poverello". Later, the Order rose against Elias's tyranny and expelled him, and the Pope also excommunicated him. He joined the entourage of the Holy Roman Emperor and became a trusted ambassador. Later, he built a convent and church above Cortona and called it San Francesco. There, eventually reconciled to the Church, he died and is buried.)

Francis brought his new Rule to the Chapter of 1221. During the meeting, he sat at the feet of Brother Elias, who, as Vicar General, was in charge. There was nothing new in the new Rule; it was just a restatement of what had gone before with passionate pleas for unity. Francis had the love and respect of all but the loyalty of only a few, and the new Rule was greeted with general dismay and murmurs of rebellion. The diplomacy and tact of Cardinal Ugolino and Brother Elias restored order and calm. The Cardinal took Francis aside and quietly suggested that the new Rule needed further amendment, and also needed to be made more concise before it was submitted to the Pope for ratification.

Francis went back to Fonte Colombo, taking Brother

Leo with him. He rewrote the Rule and sent a copy to Brother Elias. Elias did nothing with the document, and later, when asked where it was, said that someone had lost it. Francis began to despair. He knew that he had finally lost control of the Order that he had founded, his general health was poor, and his eyesight was almost gone. More and more he saw his own life as similar to the life of Jesus, and in his prayers he asked for more suffering. With some of the Brothers who had remained loyal to him, Francis moved on to Greccio. A while later, Francis wrote out his Rule again. He took it to Rome and, after modification, on 29 September 1223 it was approved by the Pope (now Honorius III) as the Regula Bullata. Francis did not wholly approve of the new Rule, and Brother Elias and some of the Provincial Ministers refused to obey it.

Francis now knew that he had done everything in his power to make the way of poverty secure. The fact that some of the Brothers disobeyed his wishes upset him. He prayed much about it, and on one occasion, deep in prayer, it seemed that Christ came and talked to him. The conversation gave him great comfort. Jesus asked, "O little poor man, why are you troubled? I have set you as the shepherd over My Brotherhood, but have you forgotten that I am its chief protector? I have chosen you, a simple, unlearned man, so men may know that the wonders you do come by grace from above, not through man. It is I who have called the Brothers, I who keep them, I who feed them. Even though some fall away, I will raise up others in their place, so that My religion shall always remain unshaken."

The Christmas Crib

Interspersed with the despair were moments of joy when the old, laughing, enthusiastic Francis broke through. As Christmas approached he had a novel idea for celebrating that joyful feast. He asked the local Lord, Giovanni da Vellita, to come and see him. Brother Giovanni (John) was a member of the Third Order of Francis and was willing to help in any way that he could. He had already given land to the Order – a mountain slope opposite Greccio, and a Franciscan hermitage had been built there. The land also had a cave, which Francis had noticed to be very much like the grotto at Bethlehem. He asked Giovanni to turn the cave into a stable, making it exactly like the stable in which Jesus had been born. He had a manger built, and on the afternoon of the service, he had an ox and an ass delivered. Invitations were sent out to all the Brothers living in the hermitages round about, and to everyone who lived in the area. On Christmas Eve hundreds of people came in torchlight processions, climbing the path to the cave, singing hymns of praise. At the service the priest used the manger as an altar, with the animals tethered on either side. Francis acted as deacon, read the Christmas gospel, and then preached to the people, explaining what was happening. He spoke tenderly and persuasively, and made the people laugh when he deliberately emphasised the first syllable of the word 'Bethlehem' as if he was a bleating lamb. Then the Mass continued and at the consecration the priest put the bread and the cup of wine on the straw in the manger. The Lord Jesus was in the manger, just as He had been over 1,200 years before.

The Christmas Day saw the Brothers at Fonte Colombo sitting down to something like a banquet, probably provided by the kindly Lord Giovanni. A bell was rung to call Francis to the dinner table. When he saw the fine meal, the table linen, the glass goblets and so on, he was bemused rather than angry. Perhaps the scene reminded him of his younger days when he was a well-off, well-dressed, well-fed young man living in Assisi. He slipped out of the room and waited until all the Brothers were seated and eating. Then he knocked on the door and was called in by the feasting friars. All turned to look at who the visitor was – it was Francis, wearing an old beggar's hat, and hobbling with the aid of a stick – "For the love of the Lord God, make an offering to this poor and infirm pilgrim," he said.

At one time, in a moment of depression, Francis wandered alone to the Carceri to find Brother Bernard, who was in retreat there. Francis could hardly see, and he was in a state of physical and mental exhaustion. He wandered round the woods calling out Bernard's name, but there was no reply. The third time he called, "Brother Bernard, come and speak to the poor, blind man." Again there was no reply. Self-pity was stopped by humour which reprimanded him: "What are you grieving at, you wretched little man? Bernard is probably speaking with God. Is he going to dismiss such a guest that he may attend a mere creature like you?" Just at that moment, Bernard came running to him. Francis lay face down on the ground and ordered Bernard, by holy obedience, to put his foot on him three times and to say, "Lie there, you boorish son of Bernardone. Vilest of creatures, why are you so proud?" 'By holy obedience' meant that Bernard had to do it, but he did it gently.

Another story says that two young Brothers travelled a long way to visit Francis, to assure him of their love and loyalty, and to ask for his blessing. When they arrived nobody knew where Francis was, because he had gone off somewhere to pray alone, and they did not know when he might return. The young Brothers were upset because they could not stay, so their hard journey had been a waste of time. "This is punishment for our sins. We are not worthy to be blessed by our Father Francis," they said as they turned to go down the mountain. Upset by their sadness, some of the Brothers decided to accompany the pilgrims down to the plain. They had all climbed down some way when they heard a shout from above – Francis was standing at the door of the hermitage. He had returned and had heard of the young Brothers' visit, and of their disappointment. The Brothers fell on their knees and Francis blessed them several times, (though he could not see them), making large, slow signs of the cross.

The Marks of Christ

In the autumn of 1224, Francis felt compelled to go to La Verna. He chose a few of his closest Brothers to go with him – Leo, Angelo, Silvester, Rufino, and Masseo. On La Verna there were rough huts and a small chapel, built on the orders of Lord Orlando of Chiusi, dedicated to Saint Mary of the Angels (named after the mother chapel of the Portiuncula). At Francis's request, a small cell was built for him under a beech tree, a short distance from the other Brothers. He wanted to be alone with God and he gave strict instructions that only Brother Leo should go near him, taking bread and water when it was thought necessary. After a few days, Francis decided to move to somewhere more remote. He said to Leo, "Go and stand at the door of the chapel, and when I call you, come to me." Francis climbed up the mountain and called for Leo, who came immediately. This operation was repeated until Leo could not hear Francis's call. At that place there was a deep and narrow ravine, and Francis decided to live there for the Michaelmas period. Together, he and Leo got a tree trunk to use as a bridge across the narrow divide. Then he called the other Brothers and showed them where he would like his cell built – in a gash in the mountainside. When that was done, Francis gave strict instructions that he was not to be disturbed; Brother Leo was to go to him once in the day, and once in the night at the time of Matins, to see if Francis wanted anything. He was to stand at the bridge and say, "Domine, labia mea aperies," the first words of Matins, 'O Lord, open my lips.' If Francis said, "Come," then Leo was to cross the bridge and they would say Matins together; if there was no reply then he was to go away.

For many days Francis wandered and meditated, one of his favourite places for meditation being in a gorge over which a huge rock, called the Sasso Spicco, juts out. He was not alone because a falcon kept him company and was a great comfort to him. Francis was nearly blind, but he delighted in the fresh smells of the shrubs and trees, and the sounds of the leaves rustling beneath his feet, the wind, and the birds, as well as the periods of silence. He felt very close to God.

The Fioretti tells us that near to the feast of the Holy Cross, Brother Leo went to visit Francis at the hour of Matins. As usual, he stopped at the bridge and called, "O Lord, open my lips," but Francis did not answer. But Leo did not go away as he had been told to do; instead he crossed the bridge to look for his master. Francis was not in his cell so Leo, guided by the light of the moon, searched the woods until he heard Francis praying out loud. "Who are you, O my most sweet God, and what am I, most vile worm and worthless servant?" At that moment Leo saw Francis surrounded by light. He decided not to disturb Francis and made to creep away. But his retreat was noisy because of dry leaves rustling underneath his feet, and he was heard.

Francis called out, "Who are you?" and ordered him to stop.

"I am Brother Leo, my Father," he answered.

"Why have you come here, Brother Little Sheep? Have I not told you not to come and watch me?"

Leo knelt down at Francis's feet and begged to be forgiven, and then asked for an explanation for what had happened. "Know, Brother Little Sheep, that when I said those words there was shown to me in my soul two lights, one of the understanding of myself, and the other of the knowledge of the Creator. . . . But take heed to yourself, Brother Little Sheep, that you watch me no more." Brother Leo then returned to the others.

During the morning of Holy Cross Day, 14 September, the day that the friars who had been sent to England heard the bells of Canterbury for the first time, Francis spent his time in meditation on the death of Jesus, possibly sitting under the great rock called the Sasso Spicco. Into his mind came the vision of Isaiah: "In the year that King Uzziah died, I saw the Lord. He was sitting on his throne, high and exalted, and his robe filled the whole Temple. Round him were flaming creatures standing, each of which had six wings. Each creature covered its face with two wings, and its body with two, and used the other two for flying. They called out to each other: 'Holy, holy, holy! The Lord Almighty is holy! His glory fills the world.' The sound of their voices made the foundation of the Temple shake, and the Temple itself was filled with smoke." Then it seemed to Francis as if a six-winged seraph was coming towards him from heaven, and at the next moment revealed itself as a figure of a man nailed onto a cross. The man's face was so full of love and pain that Francis was filled with terror; but it was also a terror mingled with exquisite joy. Jesus spoke to him and said, "Do you know, Francis, what I have done to you? I have given you the marks of my Passion so that you may be my standard-bearer." He also said other things, which Francis told no one. The vision faded and Francis saw that he had the marks of crucifixion nails in his hands and in his feet, and his side was cut as if he had been stabbed with a spear. He had received the stigmata – the five wounds of Christ, the first recorded happening. (We have the written word of Brother Elias and Brother Leo that they had seen the stigmata on Francis whilst he was alive. Brother Rufino saw the wounds, as did many others, after Francis had died. In his humility, Francis always tried to hide the wounds – he wore socks and had cloth bound round his hands.)

A little while later, Francis wrote down (in Latin) his joyful praise to God for what had happened to him on Holy Cross Day. He asked Brother Leo to bring him pen and ink and with his wounded hands wrote:

"You Lord God are holy, You are God of gods,
   only You work wonders;
You are strong, You are great, You are most high;
You are almighty, holy Father, King of heaven and
   earth.
You are three and one, Lord and God of gods.
You are good, all good, the highest good.
Lord God, living and true, You are love and
   charity;
You are wisdom, humility, patience;
You are fortitude and prudence, You are security
   and rest.
You are joy and gladness, justice and temperance.
You are our sufficient riches, You are beauty and
   gentleness.
You are our protector, our guardian and defender;
You are our refuge and strength, our faith, hope
   and charity.
You are our great sweetness, eternal life to us,
   infinite goodness,

Great and wondrous Lord God Almighty, Saviour merciful and loving."

Francis gave the parchment to Brother Leo, and on the back of it he had written a special blessing for his special companion at that special time: "The Lord bless you and keep you; the Lord show His face to you and have mercy upon you; the Lord turn His countenance to you and give you peace. The Lord bless you, Brother Leo."

It was signed with a cross. Brother Leo kept the parchment folded against his heart until he died, nearly fifty years later in 1271. (It was then given to the Brothers of the Sagro Convento in Assisi, where it can be seen today in a silver reliquary. Also on the parchment can be seen the small, neat handwriting of Brother Leo, telling the story of La Verna.)

Spiritually and mentally, Francis felt very strong, but physically he was weak. The wounds on his feet were so painful that he could not walk. However, he was determined to go on another preaching mission. Lord Orlando gave him an ass, so on 30 September he left La Verna. The last thing he did as he left the hermitage was to bless all those who were staying behind: "Farewell, Brother Masseo, farewell Angelo and Rufino. Addio, addio. Peace be with you, my dearest sons. I am going with Brother Little Sheep to Saint Mary of the Angels, and I shall never come back here again. Farewell, dearest brother falcon. I thank you for the love you bore me. Farewell, Sasso Spicco, I shall not visit you again. Farewell, little chapel of Saint Mary of the Angels. To you, Mother of the Eternal Word, I commend these my sons."

Return to Assisi – the Canticle of Brother Sun

Francis rode on the ass, which Brother Leo led down the mountain, back to the Portiuncula. As Francis passed through the villages, people ran out to see him. "Ecco il santo – Behold the saint," they shouted, and they rushed forward to kiss his bound-up hands.

There followed a time of suffering, laughter, and singing. Occasionally, Francis liked to play little tricks on the Brothers. A new cloak, which the Brothers had just given him, was handed over to a beggar whose wife had just died. Francis knew that the Brothers would buy the cloak back so he solemnly ordered the man not to give it back without being paid well. The Brothers had to pay!

In spite of his physical frailty, and ignoring those who were worried by his failing health, Francis started a new preaching mission. Eventually, however, he was ordered, gently and diplomatically, by Cardinal Ugolino, to go to the Bishop's Palace in Rieti to be examined by the best doctors available. Francis obeyed reluctantly. On the first day of his journey to Rieti he got as far as Sister Clare at Saint Damian's (a ten-minute ride). Clare was worried about Francis's health and told him to go no further. She had a wattle hut made for him in the convent garden, and there he stayed for six weeks, nursed by Brothers Leo, Masseo, Angelo, and Rufino. Clare made the invalid a pair of slippers (which can be seen at Saint Damian's to this day). There were nights of pain when Francis could not sleep. On one such night he was bothered by lots of mice running round the hut. What with the pain, and the mice, life seemed to be unfair and he began to feel sorry for himself. Realising that self-pity was a sin, Francis thought, "Now, brother, rejoice and be merry in your infirmities, for are you not as sure of the Kingdom as if you were already there?" Then he began to think about all the blessings that he had received – the sunlight, the moon and stars, the wind and the rain, the streams and lakes, and the seas. He began to think of God in the four elements of earth, air, fire and water, and as he thought he began to compose a poem in praise of the Creator God. The poem became known as "The Canticle of Brother Sun" or "The Praises of the Creatures". In the morning, Francis excitedly called the Brothers to him, and insisted that, before he forgot it, Brother Leo should write down the poem. For the first time they heard "Il Cantico di Frate Sole".

"Altissimu omnipotente Bonsignore . . .
Most high, omnipotent, good Lord God,
To You be praise and glory, honour and blessing;
Only to You, most high, do they belong,
And no man is great enough to speak of You.

Be praised, my Lord, with all Your creatures,
And most of all for Monsignor Brother Sun,
Who makes the day for us, and the light.
Fair is he, and radiant, and magnificent:
A likeness, Lord most high, of You.

Be praised, my Lord, for Sister Moon and all the
  stars.

In heaven You have set them, precious, bright and
   fair.

Be praised, my Lord, for Brother Wind
And for air and cloud, and every kind of weather
By which You give nourishment to all Your
   creatures.

Be praised, my Lord, for Sister Water,
Useful, humble, precious and clean.

Be praised, my Lord, for Brother Fire
By whom You give light at night.
Beautiful he is, and joyous, vigorous and strong.

Be praised, my Lord, for our mother, Sister Earth
Who sustains and keeps us, and produces for us
Her varied fruits, and coloured flowers, and grass.

O, praise and bless my Lord, and thankful be,
And serve Him, all, with great humility."

Francis wanted Brother Pacifico to set the poem to music, and had the idea of a group of singing and preaching Brothers travelling the world singing this song to people in the marketplaces: "The best preacher in the troupe must first proclaim the meaning of the canticle, and then all will sing it, and then the preacher must say, 'We are the minstrels of the Lord, and like other minstrels we want to be paid, but the only pay we ask from you is repentance.'" He added verses to the canticle as he felt inspired.

There had been an argument between Bishop Guido and the Chief Magistrate/Mayor. The end result had been that the Bishop had excommunicated the Mayor and Corporation and in retaliation the Mayor had forbidden any citizen to trade with the Bishop or his clergy. Francis decided to do something about the situation; he knew that God was not only in the sun and moon and stars, but was, most of all, in the charity and kindness of people. He composed a new verse to his canticle and then asked the Bishop and the Mayor to meet him in the courtyard of the Bishop's Palace, because he had something to say to both of them. The Bishop sat on his throne, with his clergy around him, at one end of the courtyard, and at the other end, some way away, the Mayor and his officials gathered. Francis had sent two friars, and one of them addressed the assembled dignitaries: "My Lord Bishop and Excellencies, your brother Francis, in his weakness, has made a praise of the Lord concerning all His creatures, and he asks you to listen to it very carefully." The Brother explained more about the Canticle and then the two friars sang it. A new verse had been added:

> "Be praised, my Lord, for those who pardon for
>   Your love,
> Who bear infirmity and tribulation.
> Blessed are those who keep themselves in peace,
> For You shall crown them, Lord most high."

Much moved by the words, the Mayor went and knelt before the Bishop and asked for his forgiveness. The Bishop got the Mayor to rise and asked for his forgiveness, saying, "My position bids me to be humble, but alas, I am quick to get angry! It is my part to ask you to forgive me." Both men embraced and gave each other the kiss of peace.

Medical Treatment

After six weeks with Sister Clare, Francis was well enough to journey on to Rieti, where he was received as an honoured guest in the Bishop's palace. Cardinal Ugolino did everything he could to make Francis comfortable, but Francis did not like living in a palace, and he asked to move to the nearest hermitage – Fonte Colombo. His request was granted. There he composed more songs, which he sent to Clare, and dictated two letters, one to the whole Order, and one to "all Christians everywhere", to be read out after his death.

The pain in Francis's eyes had gradually been getting worse, so Cardinal Ugolino and Brother Elias insisted on calling in the best doctors. One of these doctors recommended that the side of Francis's face, from jaw to eyebrow, should be cauterised with a red-hot iron. Francis asked Brother Elias to be present at the operation, but when he was late, Francis told the doctor to begin without him. The doctor put the iron into the brazier and the friars in the room all fled; when the iron was ready Francis stood up and said: "Deal courteously with me, Brother Fire, God made you beautiful, strong and useful, and I have always loved you. Be gentle with me this day." Francis blessed the doctors, who went on to cut the nerve near his eyes. One of the Brothers later remarked, "God is laying His hand on you more heavily than you deserve." Francis replied, "What a simple-minded fool you are! If I did not know you better I would have shunned your company for talking such nonsense. It is God's will that I should suffer, and there is the end of it." Later, he told the Brothers that he had felt nothing when the iron was burning the side of his face. The operation was a failure. The eyesight grew no better, and for several months Francis stayed at different places in the Rieti Valley, while other useless remedies were tried. On one occasion, Francis heard of a poor woman nearby who was suffering with the same eye disease; he sent her his cloak and some loaves of bread.

A story is told that when Francis was lying ill in the Bishop's palace and his eyes were more painful than usual, he longed to hear some music. His sight was gone, but, at least, he could still hear. He called one of the Brothers who could play the lute and asked him to "sing a cheerful song to comfort Brother Body, who is full of pain". The Brother was scandalised by the idea. It did not seem right that a friar who was very ill, and perhaps even dying, should listen to cheerful songs. People outside might hear and be shocked by such frivolous behaviour. "Let it be then, Brother. It is better to give up things than to hurt people's feelings," Francis said. In the night, Francis heard his music. As he lay awake, thinking of God's love, it seemed to him that the room was full of music. It was so good that it seemed that an angel was playing a lute. Francis spent the night in rapture, forgetting his sickness and pain. In the morning, he called the lute-playing Brother to him and said, "The Lord did not leave me comfortless. I might not hear the music of men, but in the night I heard the sound of a lute far sweeter than theirs."

Some time later, the Cardinal sent Francis to Siena,

where the air was supposed to be good for invalids and where there were many more doctors. But Francis grew worse, coughing up blood. Afraid that Francis was dying, the Brothers gathered round his bed and asked him to bless them. Francis called for Brother Benedict of Pirato, who was acting as his secretary at the time, and said to him, "Write that I bless my Brothers who are in the Order, and all those who shall come into it, even to the end of the world. And since, because of my weakness, I may not speak much, I make plain my desire to all my Brothers present and to come, in these brief words: that they shall always love one another as I have loved them, that they shall always love and observe our lady Poverty, and that they shall remain faithful servants of our holy Mother Church."

Return to Assisi for the Last Time

When Brother Elias saw how weak and ill Francis was, he was determined to get him back to Assisi. Francis wanted to die "at home" and Elias wanted to make sure that the body of the man who was already called a saint should belong to the Order he ruled, and to no one else. So he arranged that the journey back to Assisi be as secret as possible, and that as soon as the group drew near to the city, soldiers should guard it until it reached Bishop Guido's palace. Crowds of people streamed out of Assisi to welcome Francis back and a triumphant procession escorted the litter to the Bishop's palace. Francis was guarded day and night by soldiers and citizens.

Francis was now in constant pain and he had developed dropsy as well. To take his mind off the pain, he would sing for much of the day, and during the night too. He often asked the Brothers to join him in the singing. Elias thought that such behaviour was unseemly and asked Francis to stop: "Dearest Brother, I am greatly consoled and edified by all the gladness which you show for yourself and for your fellows in your ailments. But though the men of this city venerate you as a holy man, yet because they believe you close to death, hearing these praises sung day and night, they may say within themselves, 'Why does this man show such light-heartedness who is near to death? Surely he should be thinking of death?'" Francis's answer was brief and simple: "Allow me, Brother, to rejoice in my Lord, both in His glory and in my infirmities, since by the grace of His Spirit, I feel so united to Him that I need to sing."

In the last months, Francis found eating difficult, but just occasionally he had a whim for some sort of food. During one long night he could not sleep, so he asked the Brother who was at his bedside if he could get him some parsley. Perhaps the Brother was sleepy, perhaps he did not want to go out into the garden in the dark, or perhaps Francis was over-sensitive, but he saw a momentary creasing of the Brother's brow. That reaction to his request worried Francis, so for the rest of the night he began to think that he had become unreasonable and selfish, and that his own behaviour was making his Brothers commit the sin of impatience. Audibly he prayed, "O God, do not let me be to them a cause of selfishness and sin." In the morning he called the Brothers to him and said: "Dearest Brothers and my little sons, do not let it weary you to labour for me in my sickness, because the Lord will return to you the fruit of your works for one of His humble servants. If you spend yourselves on me now, I think that the Lord will be your debtor on my account."

"Be praised, my Lord, for Sister Death"

One day Francis could be much better, on the next day he could be haemorrhaging. The doctor attending him was an old friend called Bongiovanni, and Francis asked him how long he had to live. "Well, Father," he answered, "I see no reason why, if God is willing, this sickness should not pass away in time." Francis smiled, realising the ambiguity of the answer, and pressed the doctor for the truth. "Now come, Bembegnato," he said, using a nickname, "I am not a cuckoo, and I am not afraid of death. In the mercy of God I feel so close to Him that it means little to me whether I live or die." Bongiovanni admitted that Francis's illness was incurable and that he would probably live until the end of September, or the beginning of October. Francis turned away from the doctor and said, "Welcome, my Sister Death." When the doctor had left Francis sent for Brother Leo and Brother Angelo and asked them to sing "The Praises of the Creatures". Francis did not join in the singing, and in the silence after the canticle had finished he said, "I have composed a new verse:

> Be praised, my Lord, for Sister Death,
> From whom no man living can escape.
> Alas for those who die in mortal sin,

But happy they who find themselves within Your
   will,
On them the second death can work no harm.
Praise you and bless my Lord, and do Him service
   due,
With humblest thanks for all He has done for you!"

Then he said, "I would like to die at the Portiuncula."

Brother Elias organised a large escort of soldiers to take Francis to the Portiuncula. On the way there, Francis asked to stop, and that his stretcher be turned to face towards Assisi. He raised his hand and blessed the city he could not see: "You are blessed of the Lord, O city, because through you many souls shall be saved. I beg You, O Lord Jesus Christ, that You be always mindful of Your own most abundant tenderness which You have shown forth in her, that she may ever be the place and dwelling of those who acknowledge You truly and glorify Your name for ever and ever. Amen." Then he asked to be carried on. They passed the leper hospital of San Salvatore and came, eventually, to the Portiuncula, a collection of buildings now. Francis was put in an isolated cell known as the Infirmary.

Francis asked that a message be sent to the Lady Giacoma da Settisoli, who lived in Rome, asking her to come and be with him. Francis and some of the Brothers had often stayed with her when they had been in Rome and called her "Brother Giacoma". He asked that she should bring a shroud, some candles, and some of the marzipan cakes that she used to make for him, which he loved so much. As the messenger prepared to leave the Lady Giacoma turned up at the gate with her sons, servants, and nearly all the things that Francis had requested – a grey tunic made from the lamb that he had once given her (saved from the butcher's some years before), a cloth to cover his face, some incense, and some candles. "Bring her in, for the Rule concerning women is not for Brother Giacoma," Francis said. She rushed into the infirmary, fell on her knees, and buried her face in the bedclothes at Francis's feet, insisting that she would not leave him until all was over. Francis promised that she could stay until the day after he died. (After his death, she came and lived in Assisi and was very good to Brother Leo, and to the other Brothers who remained loyal to Francis's ideals, who were being persecuted by Brother Elias. There is also a story told that when Brother Leo lay dying, nearly fifty years later, an old woman called Brother Giacoma nursed him to the end and closed his eyes after he had died. When Brother Giacoma died, the Brothers buried her near the high altar of the lower church of San Francesco. When the crypt was reorganised in the twentieth century, her remains were moved into the crypt, opposite the body of Francis. In the four corners of the crypt lie the remains of Brothers Leo, Angelo, Rufino and Masseo, guarding their Father Francis still.)

Sister Clare was not allowed to visit Francis because her Order was enclosed, but she sent him messages assuring him of her love and prayers, and the love and prayers of all her Sisters. Francis dictated a letter to her: "I, little Brother Francis, desire to follow the life and poverty of my Lord Jesus Christ, and of His holy Mother, and to persevere in it to the end. And I beg you, my ladies, and I give you counsel that you live always in this most holy life and poverty. And be very careful, lest by the teaching or counsel of any other you depart from it."

Francis also instructed that when he had died his body should be taken to Assisi by way of Saint Damian's, and put before the Sisters' door, so that they might see him one last time and say goodbye.

When he was close to death, Francis asked that he should be placed on the floor of the Infirmary, with all his clothes removed. Lying on the ground, he accepted from the Father Guardian a tunic, a pair of breeches, a rope belt, and a cowl, given to him with the words, "Know that these things are only lent to you by me, and you have no right of property in them." Francis accepted the clothes as a loan – now he was ready to die, owning nothing at all. He had written his will which was a fairly rambling account of his life, emphasising poverty, and stating how he believed the Brothers of his Order ought to live. He was afraid that Brother Elias would lead them away from the poverty ordered in the Gospels. The Brothers should only have one tunic, a rope belt, and breeches. They should work with their hands to gain a living, and if they had to beg then they should salute people lovingly with the words, "The Lord give you peace." They should not own churches or have stone houses built for them, but if they did then they were to live in them as pilgrims and not as owners. They should respect all priests and be loyal to the Pope and to the Church, and should especially show respect for the Holy Eucharist. They were never to leave the Portiuncula. Nothing Francis had written was new; it was simply what he had always believed and lived. "This is not a new Rule I am giving you, it is but a remembrance," he said.

On Thursday, 1 October 1226, the Brothers gathered round Francis's bed because they realised that his death was near. They sang to him, and he joined in the singing when he had the strength to do so. At one time he was brought some food which he tasted and then said, "This is something that Bernard likes." He called Bernard to him and shared the food. As the senior Brother present, Bernard asked Francis to forgive them all for their failures and to bless them. Francis replied, "See, my son, God is calling me. I forgive all my Brothers, whether present or absent, all their offences and faults, and as far as I can I absolve them. And I bless them as much as I can, and more than I can. Tell them this everywhere, and bless them all from me." Then he placed his hand upon the head of each friar present and gave him a private blessing. Being blind, he could not tell one Brother from another, and when he had his hand on Giles's head he thought that he was blessing Bernard. He asked Bernard to come near and he blessed him: "You are my firstborn, chosen to give an example and follow Christ in holy poverty. You gave not only all you had for the love of Christ, but you also offered yourself, a sacrifice of sweetness. Blessed are you by our Lord Jesus Christ, and by me, His little poor servant, with everlasting blessings. Be you blessed, walking and standing, watching and sleeping, living and dying." Then he asked Brother Leo to write: "I wish and command that all Brothers in the whole Order shall honour Bernard as if he were myself, for he was the first who came to me, and gave his goods to the poor." Francis also blessed Brother Elias, the head of the Order who had caused much anguish because although he loved Francis, he did not understand him: "I bless you, my son, in all things and through all things. By your hands has the Most High increased the number of Brothers. In you do I bless them all. My God bless you in heaven and on earth. I bless you as I can and more than I can. May God remember your work and reward you."

The Brothers stayed with Francis all night, and as the

first light of Friday came into the hut, he said, "I would like you to bring a loaf and we will break it and eat it together as our Master did the Thursday before he died." Francis could not tell day from night, so they gently told him that it was Friday morning. "I thought it was still Thursday," he said. A loaf was brought and Francis broke it into pieces and gave each Brother a piece, which they all ate to show their common love. "Now read me the Gospel for Maundy Thursday," Francis asked. A book of Gospel readings was brought and one of the Brothers read the story of the Last Supper. For the rest of that Friday, and on the Saturday, Francis grew weaker and weaker. Just as the sun was going down on Saturday, 3 October 1226, everyone heard the larks (Francis's favourite birds) singing in the last of the sunlight. Francis began to sing Psalm 142 and the Brothers joined in:

"I called to the Lord with my voice; I make my supplication.
I poured out my complaints; I tell Him all my troubles.
When my spirit was overwhelmed, then You know what I should do.
In the path where I walk, my enemies have hidden a trap for me.
When I look on my right hand, I see that there is no one to help me,
No one to protect me. No one cares for me.
Lord, I called to You for help; You, Lord, are my refuge;
You are all I want in this life.
Hear my cry for help, for I am sunk in despair.
Save me from my persecutors; they are stronger than I am.

Set my soul free from prison; that I may praise
Your name:
The good shall surround me, because You have
dealt bountifully with me."

These were Francis's last words. The Brothers saw that he was dead, a look of happiness and peace on his face. In the silence the larks were still singing.

Tradition says that as he lay dying, Francis asked to be buried on the 'Collis Infernus', a hill just outside Assisi, where criminals were executed and buried. His wish was not granted. His body was taken in procession to the church of San Giorgio, stopping on the way outside the convent of Saint Damian's, so that Clare and her Sisters could say their last goodbye. He was buried in the church and his body stayed there for two years, after which, against the wishes of the townspeople, it was moved to the huge new church built on the orders of Brother Elias. So that the remains should not be moved again, Elias had them hastily and stealthily buried deep down in the solid rock. The exact place he kept a secret. (The remains were discovered in 1818 and were reburied in an ornate tomb. In 1932 they were placed in a simple tomb, much more in keeping with the Franciscan ideal.)

In 1228, just two years after Francis's death, Cardinal Ugolino, who had now become Pope Gregory IX, declared Francis to be a saint. In the Piazza San Giorgio, his eyes full of tears, he spoke movingly of his love for Saint Francis of Assisi – the poor little rich man of God.

Bibliography

The author gratefully acknowledges the following sources for material:

The Little Flowers of St. Francis, trans. T. Okey (London: Temple Press, 1910).
Salter, E. G., *The Legend of the Three Companions*, trans *Legenda Trium Sociorum* (First printed 1768, first complete edition Rome 1899, transl. E.G. Salter London, Dent Temple Classics 1902).
Celano, Thomas of, *Life* of St. Francis, trans. A. G. F. Howell (London: Temple Press, 1910).
Leo, Brother, The Mirror of Perfection (Speculum Perfectionis), trans. R. Steele (London: Temple Press, 1910).
Chesterton, G. K., *St. Francis of Assisi* (R. A. Kessinger Publishing Co, 2003).
Farmer, D. H., *The Oxford Dictionary of Saints* (Oxford: Oxford University Press, 2004).
Grierson, E. W., *The Story of St. Francis of Assisi* (London: A. R. Mowbray, 1912).
Cuthbert, Fr., *Life of St. Francis of Assisi* (Details unknown).
Duncan Jones, C. M., *The Lord's Minstrel* (Cambridge: W. Heffer & Sons Ltd, 1927).
Payne, R., *The Fathers of the Western Church* (London: W Heinemann Ltd, 1952).
Webling, P., *Saints and Their Stories* (London: Nisbet & Co Ltd, n.d.).
Gurney Salter, E., *The Life of Saint Francis*, trans. (London: Everymans Library, 1941).
Rolt-Wheeler, E., *Women of the Cell and Cloister* (London: Methuen & Co Ltd, 1913).

St Francis of Assisi

Clarke, C. P. S., *Every Man's Book of Saints* (London: A. R. Mowbray, 1914).
Raymond, E. *In the Steps of St Francis* (London: Rich and Cowan, 1938).

Prayers Attributed to Saint Francis

O Almighty God, eternal, righteous, and merciful, give us poor sinners to do for Your sake all that we know of Your will, and to will always that which pleases You; so that inwardly purified, enlightened, and kindled by the fire of Your Holy Spirit, we may follow in the steps of Your well-beloved Son, our Lord Jesus Christ. Amen.

We beseech You, O Lord, to guide Your Church with Your perpetual governance that it may walk warily in times of quiet, and boldly in times of trouble, through Jesus Christ our Lord. Amen.

O Lord, make us instruments of Your peace.
Where there is hatred, may we bring love;
Where there is injury, forgiveness;
Where there is discord, harmony;
Where there is despair, hope;
Where there is sadness, joy.
May we ourselves
Seek to understand rather than to be understood,
To console rather than to be consoled,
To love rather than to be loved.
For it is in giving that we receive,
It is in forgiving that we are forgiven,
It is through dying that we are born to eternal life
In Jesus Christ our Lord. Amen.